Blairsville Junior High School
Blairsville, Pennsylvania

DATE DUE			3236
DEC 18			
MAR 5			
DEC 2 2			
JAN 2 0			
NOV 10 '80			
NOV 08 1998			
JAN 2 1 1998			
GAYLORD			PRINTED IN U.S.A.

3236

DAVIS, MARILYN

MUSIC DICTIONARY

Blairsville Junior High School
Blairsville, Pennsylvania

Music Dictionary

Music Dictionary

by Marilyn Kornreich Davis

in collaboration with Arnold Broido

illustrated by Winifred Greene

DOUBLEDAY & COMPANY, INC., GARDEN CITY, NEW YORK

Library of Congress Card Number 54-9837

To my husband, my parents and my grandparents

MARILYN KORNREICH DAVIS

AUTHOR'S NOTE

The purpose of this book is to define in simple language, with numerous practical illustrations and examples, those musical terms and expressions which the student of music is most likely to encounter. It has been kept as clear as the concepts will allow, and the most commonly used terms have the simplest definitions so that the youngest musicians will be able to understand them. At the same time, the material is so worded as to be useful to anyone interested in music.

It should be pointed out that some of the definitions do not include all meanings of the words or phrases, and from time to time current musicological study may bring a new understanding of some of the terms. The definitions in this book are mainly traditional and have been presented in what is believed to be their most useful form.

A

A Pitch name. The A above middle C, vibrating 440 times a second, is the standard pitch for American music and instruments.

On the staff: On the keyboard:

a battuta (IT. ah baht-too′tah) In strict time; return to strict time.

absolute music Music composed simply as music, without a program, story, etc.; the opposite of program music, which is based on a story, event, picture, etc.

a cappella (IT. ah cahp-pel′lah) Unaccompanied choral singing; from the Italian word meaning "chapel." Music usually written for the choir of a chapel.

a capriccio (IT. ah cah-pree′choh) To be played freely, fancifully, capriciously.

accelerando (IT. aht-chel-ay-rahn′doh) Growing faster; accelerating. Abbreviation: *accel.*

accent Stress, emphasis.
These are accent signs:

acciacatura (IT. atch-yac-cah-too′rah) A musical ornament. The acciacatura is a rapid grace note one half step below the principal note. It has no time value, being played together with its principal note, then immediately released. Acciacatura comes from the Italian word meaning "to crush." See **ornaments.**

accidental Chromatic alteration not found in the key signature.
These are the signs:

    sharp ♯   double sharp ×
    flat ♭   double flat ♭♭
    natural ♮

accompaniment Provides the background for a musical theme; from "accompany," which means "go with."

Theme:

Accompaniment:

accordion A portable musical instrument. Consists of a bellows for pumping air through its reeds, a piano keyboard for melody notes, and buttons for bass notes and chords. There are two sets of reeds, one that plays when the bellows is being opened, the other when it is being closed. See **concertina, wind instruments.**

acoustics (a-coo′stix) The science of sound.

adagio (IT. ah-dah′jo) Slowly; slower than andante, faster than largo.

adaptation Arrangement of a musical composition.

ad libitum (LAT.) At will. Means that the performer may:
1. change the rhythm.
2. include or leave out a voice or instrumental part.
3. include or leave out the passage (often a cadenza).
4. add a cadenza.
Abbreviation: *ad lib.*

affabile (IT. ah-fah′bee-lay) In a pleasing and graceful manner.

affettuoso (IT. ah-fet-tu-oh′soh) With emotion, warmth, tenderness.

agilmente (IT. ah-jeel-men′tay) Lightly, lively.

agitato (IT. ah-gee-tah′toh) Excited, agitated.

agréments (FR. ah-gray-mah[n]) Musical ornaments. See **ornaments.**

air Tune, melody, song.

Alberti bass A bass figure of broken chords. The Alberti bass is named after Domenico Alberti (born 1710), who used bass figures of this kind in his sonatas:

al fine (IT. ahl fee′nay) To the end.

alla (IT. ahl′lah) To the, at the, in the, etc.; in the style of.

alla breve (IT. bray′vay) 2/2 time; a half note receives one beat. There are two beats in each measure. Alla breve is indicated by:

allegretto (IT. ahl-lay-gret'toh) Lively; faster than andante, slower than allegro.

allegrissimo (IT. ahl-lay-gree'see-moh) Very rapid.

allegro (IT. ahl-lay'groh) Lively, brisk; faster than allegretto, slower than presto.

allemanda (IT. ah-lay-mahn'dah)
allemande (FR. ahl-mahnd)

1. Late sixteenth century—a German dance in duple time (two beats to the measure).

2. Late seventeenth century—the allemande was no longer danced and became part of the suite. It was in 4/4 time, with a short upbeat and frequent running figures.

3. Late eighteenth century—in South Germany the allemande appeared as a quick waltz-like dance in 3/4 or 3/8 time.

alla marcia (IT. mar'chee-ah) In march style.

alla militare (IT. mee-lee-tah'ray) In military style.

allargando (IT. ahl-lar-gahn'doh) Growing slower, broader, often with a crescendo. Abbreviation: *allarg.*

alla russa (IT. roo'sah) In Russian style.

alla turca (IT. toor'cah) In Turkish style. The last movement of Mozart's Sonata in A (Koechel 331) is headed "Alla Turca."

alla zingara (IT. tsin'gah-rah) In gypsy style.

all' ottava (IT. aw-tah'vah) See *ottava*

altissimo (IT. ahl-tees'see-moh) Highest.

alto High.
1. Female voice lower than soprano; contralto.

Range:

2. Next to highest part in a four-part chorus (soprano, alto, tenor, bass).
3. Members of the instrumental families, such as: alto clarinet, alto horn, alto saxophone, etc.

alto clef C clef on the third line of the staff:

Middle C

Viola music is written in this clef. See **clef** 2.

amabile (IT. ah-mah'bee-lay) Sweet, tender, gentle.

andante (IT. ahn-dahn'tay) Walking speed, flowing; slower than allegretto, faster than adagio.

anglaise (FR. ahn-glez) A French dance form based on the English country dance; used in the French ballets of the late seventeenth century; also found in the eighteenth-century suite.

ANGLAISE   Johann Sebastian Bach
Allegro

animato (IT. ahn-ee-mah'toh) With spirit; animated.
ansioso (IT. ahn-see-oh'soh) With anxiety; hesitation.
a piacere (IT. ah pee-aht-chay'ray) At pleasure, same as *ad libitum*. See **ad libitum**.
appassionato (IT. ahp-pahs-see-o-nah'toh) With passion, emotion.
appena (IT. ah-pay'nah) Hardly, scarcely.
appoggiatura (IT. ahp-podg-ah-too'rah) A musical ornament; from the Italian word *appoggiare,* meaning "to lean on." There are two types of appoggiatura:

1. Long appoggiatura, now seldom used. It was written in this way:

Allegretto   Wolfgang Amadeus Mozart (b. 1756)

and played like this:

2. Short appoggiatura, grace note. It is written in this way:

It is played very swiftly and is part of the time value of the note to which it is attached. The grace note is usually played slightly before the beat in music composed after 1800.

a quatre mains (FR. ah cahtr mah[n])
a quattro mani (IT. ah cwah'troh mah'nee) For four hands.

arco (IT. ahr'coh) Bow of a stringed instrument. Arco, used after a pizzicato (plucked) passage, means that the notes following are to be bowed.

aria (IT. ah'ree-ah) Song with instrumental accompaniment. The aria appears in elaborate form in operas, cantatas, and oratorios.

arpeggiando (IT. ar-ped-jahn'doh) Playing broken chords in harp style.

arpeggio (IT. ar-ped'joh) Broken chord; from the Italian word *arpeggiare,* meaning "to play a harp."

It is written in this way:

and played like this:

assai (IT. ah-sah'ee) Very. *Allegro assai* means "very fast."

assez (FR. ah-say) Fairly. *Assez vite* means "fairly quick."

a tempo (IT. ah tem'poh) In time; return to normal or previous speed.

attacca (IT. aht-tah'cah) Continue without a pause; instantly.

augmented intervals See **interval**.

aumentando (IT. ah-oo-main-tahn'doh) Crescendo; increasing in loudness.

autoharp A zither on which chords are played by pressing buttons that allow the desired strings to sound. See **zither**.

authentic cadence See **cadence**.

avec (FR. ah-vek) With. *Avec âme* means "with soul."

B

B Pitch name.

On the staff:

On the keyboard:

bagatelle (FR.) A trifle; a short, simple piece, usually for piano.

bagpipe Ancient wind instrument. The performer blows into a pipe leading to the windbag from which air is squeezed into reed pipes. One pipe, the chanter, has finger holes, and is used to play the melody. The other pipes, called drones, continuously sound one tone each. Many different types of bagpipe may still be found today throughout the world.
See **musette** 1.

ballad Song. Ballad comes from the Latin word *ballare*, meaning "to dance." Originally it was a dancing song, later becoming a vocal solo, often telling a story.

ballade (FR. bah-lahd)
1. A form of poetry and music popular in the Middle Ages, sung by trouvères (French poet-musicians).

Richard Cour-de-Lion (b. 1157)

Ja nun hons pris ne di- ra sa rai- son

2. Romantic and lyrical piano pieces of the nineteenth century composed in a free style.

Moderato   Frédéric Chopin (b. 1810)

ballet (FR. bah-lay) A formal performance by a group of dancers, usually with costumes, scenery, and musical accompaniment. There is a complete set of body movements that form the fundamental technique of ballet. Ballets are often used in operas for interludes, seldom as part of the story.

band An instrumental group
See **brass band, military band.**

banjo A fretted, stringed instrument of the guitar family. The banjo has a long neck, and usually five strings, which are strummed with the fingers. The body is like a tambourine with an open back.

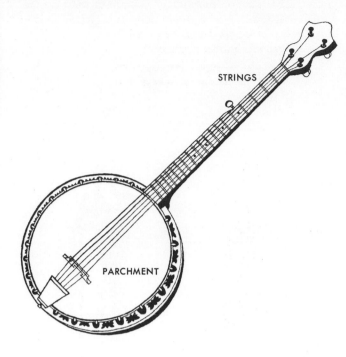

STRINGS

PARCHMENT

bar
1. A measure.
2. Term used for bar line. See **bar line.**

barcarole
1. Song of the Venetian gondoliers; from the Italian word *barca,* which means "boat."

2. A piece imitating Venetian boat songs.

Barcaroles are in 6/8 or 12/8 time, and contain accompaniments that imitate the rocking of a boat.

baritone
1. Male voice lower than tenor and higher than bass; from the Greek word *barys,* meaning "heavy" or "low."
This is the range of the baritone voice:

2. Brass wind instrument. See **euphonium.**

bar line Vertical line that divides the measures.

Bar line:

See **double bar.**

baroque (ba-roke') Music of the period from 1600 to 1750 which started with the birth of opera and oratorio (Monteverdi and Schütz) and was climaxed by the music of Bach and Handel.

bass
1. Lowest male voice.
This is the range of the bass voice:

2. Lowest part in a composition; from the Greek word *basis,* meaning "foundation."
3. Members of the instrument families, such as bass clarinet, bass drum, bass viol, etc.

bass clef
The F clef on the fourth line of the staff. The bass clef in its present form has developed out of the letter F. See **clef** 1.

basso (IT. bahs'soh)
1. Low, bass.
2. Bass voice.

basso buffo (IT. bahs'soh boo'foh) Singer of comic bass operatic roles.

bassoon Double-reed woodwind instrument, the bass of the oboe family. The lengthy tube is doubled back upon itself to reduce its height, which is a little over four feet. Each register has its own tone quality, the lowest often being used for comic effects.
This is the range of the bassoon:

basso ostinato (IT. bahs'soh o-stee-nah'toe) A short phrase of four to eight measures, which is repeated over and over, serving as a bass line:

The basso ostinato is also called "ground bass" because it provides the groundwork or accompaniment for a melody.

baton (FR. bah-toh[n]) Conductor's stick; used to beat time. The baton is made of tapered wood, or other light material.

beat Pulse of each measure.
4/4 time contains four beats or pulses in each measure.
2/4 time contains two beats or pulses in each measure.

bebop See **jazz** 5.

bell
1. Musical instrument consisting of a hollow body that sounds a definite pitch when struck.
See **campanella, carillon, chimes.**
2. Bell-shaped opening of wind instruments.

bell lyre See **glockenspiel** 2.

berceuse (FR. bare-seuz) A cradle song or lullaby; usually in 6/8 time with an accompaniment that resembles the rocking movement of a cradle.

ben, bene (IT. ben, bay'nay) Well. *Ben marcato* means "well marked."

bergamasca (IT. bair-gah-mah'scah)
1. Dance, sometimes with words, popular in the sixteenth and seventeenth centuries among the peasants of Bergamo, Italy, where it originated.
2. The nineteenth-century bergamasca is a rapid dance in 6/8 time, resembling the tarantella.
See **tarantella.**

binary (by'ner-ee) Two-part. Binary form has two sections, with each section usually repeated.
See **form** 1.

blues See **jazz** 2.

bolero A lively Spanish national dance in 3/4 time. The bolero contains many difficult steps and movements, and is accompanied by castanets held by the dancers. It is believed to have been created by Sebastián Cerezo of Cádiz, Spain, about 1780.
This is a typical bolero rhythm:

boogie-woogie See **jazz** 3.

bore The inside measurements of the tube of a wind instrument.
1. Conical bore: widens gradually and continuously from the mouthpiece to the bell as in the cornet, baritone, etc.
2. Cylindrical bore: the sides of the tube are parallel for most of the length of the instrument, widening only near the bell as in the trumpet, trombone, etc.

bouffe (FR. boof) Comic.

bourdon (FR. boor-doh[n])
1. A long, low tone or repeated bass, similar to the drone of a bagpipe. See **bagpipe, pedal point.**
2. Deep-sounding 16- or 32-foot stop on the organ.

bourrée (FR. boo-ray) A rapid dance of French origin; in duple time (two beats to the measure), with a single upbeat. The bourrée was popular in France in the seventeenth century, and was originally a peasant dance. Later it sometimes appeared in the suite.
See **suite** 1.

"BOURRÉE" FROM THE FRENCH SUITE NO. 6

bow Used to set the strings in motion on all instruments of the violin and viol families. The violin bow consists of an inward curving stick to which is attached horsehair. A screw, called the nut, pulls back the frog, which tightens the hair. Rosin is rubbed onto the hair so that friction will cause the strings to vibrate as the bow is drawn across them.

The smaller the instrument, the longer the bow; the violin bow is the longest, the bass bow is the shortest. The name "bow" comes from the resemblance of the early bows to the archer's bow.

brass band A small instrumental group consisting of brass and percussion.

brass family Instruments made of brass or other metal, part of the wind family.

The members of the brass family are: bugle, cornet, trumpet, alto horn (mellophone), French horn, baritone (euphonium), trombone, and tuba.

TROMBONE

FRENCH HORN

CORNET

SOUSAPHONE

bravura (IT. brah-voo'rah) With spirit, brilliance, boldness.

break See **jazz** 2.

brillante (IT. breel-lahn'tay) Showy, brilliant.

brioso (IT. bree-oh'soh) With fire, spirit.

brusco (IT. broo'scoh) Rough, brusque.

buffa (IT. boo'fah) Comic.

bugle A brass wind instrument with cup mouthpiece, without valves. Only eight notes are possible on the bugle, these being the overtone series. These notes are the basis of all military calls. See **overtone series**.

burlesca (IT. boor-les'cah) Comic, burlesque.

C

C Pitch name.
On the staff:

On the keyboard:

cadence The chords at the end of a phrase, section, or piece that suggest the completion of a musical thought.

There are various types of cadences:

1. Perfect cadence—can complete a musical composition satisfactorily. The tonic is the top voice of the final chord.

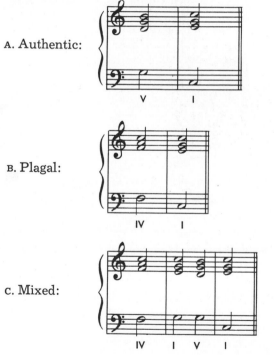

A. Authentic:

V   I

B. Plagal:

IV   I

C. Mixed:

IV   I   V   I

2. Imperfect, or half cadence—the I chord is followed by the V chord.

3. Deceptive, or interrupted cadence—the second of the two chords is an unexpected chord:

V   VI

cadenza (IT. cah-den′dzah) A brilliant virtuoso passage, usually found at the close of a vocal solo, or as a solo part of a concerto.

calando (IT. cah-lahn′doh) Growing softer and usually slower.

calcando (IT. cahl-cahn′doh) Quickening; from the Italian word meaning "trampling."

calmando (IT. cahl-mahn′doh) Growing quieter, calming.

calmato (IT. cahl-mah′toh) Peaceful, serene, calm.

calore (IT. cah-loh′ray) Passion, warmth.

campana (IT. cahm-pah′nah) Bell. See **carillon, bell.**

campanella (IT. cahm-pah-nel′lah) Little bell.

canon A strict form of musical composition in which all parts and voices have the same melody, each starting at a different time; a round. See **round.**
See example below.

cantabile (IT. cahn-tah′bee-lay) In a singing style; from the Italian word *cantare*, meaning "to sing."

cantando (IT. cahn-tahn′doh) See **cantabile.**

cantata (IT. cahn-tah′tah) Vocal work containing a number of movements such as arias, recitatives, duets, and choruses based on religious, lyrical, or dramatic subjects; from the Italian word *cantare*, meaning "to sing." Johann Sebastian Bach composed nearly three hundred church cantatas.

CANON COMPOSED ABOUT 1310   "SUMER IS ICUMEN IN"

first voice

second voice

third voice

14

cantilena (IT. cahn-tee-lay'nah) A flowing melodic phrase played or sung in a smooth vocal style.

cantus firmus (LAT.) Fixed melody; a melody to which contrapuntal voices are added according to fixed rules. See **counterpoint.**

Antonio de Cabozon (b. 1510)

"AVE MARIS STELLA"

capo (IT. cah'po) Beginning. *Da capo* means "from the beginning." Abbreviation: *D.C.*
Da capo al fine means "from the beginning to the end."
Da capo al segno means "from the beginning to the sign." The sign may be this: 𝄋 or this: ⊕

capriccio (IT. cahp-ree'choh) An instrumental composition in a free or unconventional form, often lively.

carillon (car'il-on) A chromatic set of bells sounded by means of a keyboard or a clockwork mechanism. The carillon, usually hung in the tower of a church or special bell tower, has a compass of two to four octaves. The larger sets have as many as seventy bells. See **bell** 1.

carol A traditional song heard at Christmas and Easter.

castanets A pair of hollow shells of wood or ivory hinged together by a string with which the player holds them in his hand. Castanets are struck together to mark the rhythm of such popular Spanish dances as the bolero and fandango.

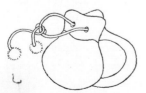

c clef See **clef** 2.
cédez (FR. say-day) Slower.

celesta (IT. chel-es'tah) A set of tuned metal bars similar to the glockenspiel, but with the addition of wooden resonators. A piano keyboard operates the hammers which strike the bars.

cello (IT. chel'loh) Abbreviation for violoncello. See **violoncello.**

cembalo (IT. chem'bah-loh) The Italian word meaning "dulcimer" which, by usage, came to mean harpsichord instead.

chaconne (FR. shak-on) and **passacaglia** (IT. pahs-sah-cahl'yah) These two dance-forms are very much alike. Both are usually in triple time (three beats to the measure), and are variations on a ground bass. See **ground bass.**

J. C. F. Fischer (b. 1650?)

"CHACONNE," "MELPOMENE" SUITE

chalumeau (FR. shah-luh-moh)
1. An ancient wind instrument of the single reed type, having a cylindrical tube with tone holes, but no keys. The word *chalumeau* comes from the Latin word for reed. This instrument is an ancestor of the clarinet.
2. The low register of the modern clarinet. See **clarinet**.

chamber music Instrumental music in which each performer has a different part, unlike orchestral music in which there are often several performers for each part. Chamber music is classified according to the number of performers:

trio—three players	sextet—six players
quartet—four players	septet—seven players
quintet—five players	octet—eight players

The string quartet is an important form of chamber music, and is composed of two violins, a viola and a cello. The string trio is composed purely of stringed instruments. If one of the strings is omitted and a piano is added, it is a piano trio; if a horn is added, it is a horn trio.

chanson (FR. shahn-soh[n]) Song.

chant A sacred song in free rhythm, unaccompanied.

chimes A set of tuned metal tubes hung from a frame. The chimes are struck at the upper (closed) end with a hammer, and are used to produce bell effects.

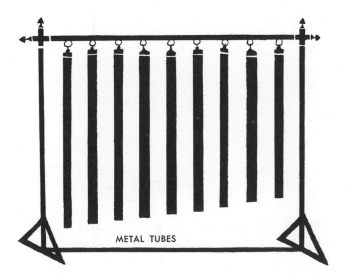

METAL TUBES

choir (quire) A group of singers or instruments; chorus.
choral (caw'ral) Relates to a chorus or choir.
chorale (caw-ral') Hymn tune.

chord (cord) Two or more tones played together.

chorus (caw'rus)
1. A group of singers.
2. Music for a group of singers.
3. The repeated section of a song, following the verse.

chromatic
1. A chromatic scale consists entirely of half steps, containing all the twelve tones within an octave.

2. Relates to accidentals not included in the key signature.
These are chromatic signs:

sharp	♯	double sharp	𝄪
flat	♭	double flat	♭♭
natural	♮		

MOUTHPIECE

BELL

clarinet   A woodwind instrument with a single reed. The clarinet consists of a cylindrical tube with a mouthpiece at one end and a bell at the other. The reed is attached to the mouthpiece with a metal band, or ligature. The tube has tone holes and keys which make it possible to play the complete chromatic scale. See **chalumeau.**

1. The B flat clarinet is a transposing instrument.

This is its written range:

This is the actual sound:

2. The A clarinet is slightly larger than the B flat clarinet, and is pitched one half step lower. It is sometimes used in place of the B flat clarinet as it is easier to play in certain keys.

3. E flat alto clarinet—pitched a perfect fifth below the B flat clarinet. It has an upturned metal bell and a metal crook to which the mouthpiece is attached. The E flat alto clarinet is a transposing instrument.

This is its written range:

This is the actual sound:

4. B flat bass clarinet—pitched one octave below the B flat clarinet. It looks like a large alto clarinet. The B flat bass clarinet is a transposing instrument.

This is its written range:

This is the actual sound:

See **transposing instruments.**

clarion
1. A shrill 4-foot organ reed stop.
2. A small, shrill English trumpet, no longer in use.

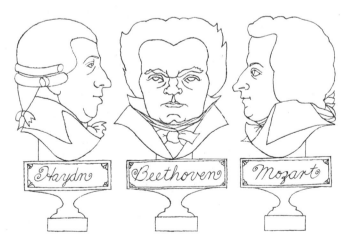

classical music   Music of the period during which such composers as Haydn, Mozart, and Beethoven lived (from about 1750 to 1830). Classical music is distinctly different in form and style from the free, exaggerated, and passionate music that flowed from the pens of such composers as Chopin and Liszt (who lived during what is known as the romantic period, which followed). The most important development of the classical period was the sonata form, on which the classical symphony, and much of the chamber music of the time, was based. See **sonata form.**

Haydn   Beethoven   Mozart

clavecin (FR. clahv-sa[n]) The French word for harpsichord.

clavichord An early stringed keyboard instrument. The strings are stretched across the length of the oblong wooden box. At the end of each key is a small brass wedge, or tangent. When the key is struck, this tangent rises and strikes the string, causing it to sound. The clavichord was the first keyboard instrument on which it was possible to play soft and loud by changing the pressure on the keys. The tone quality of the clavichord is delicate and beautiful.

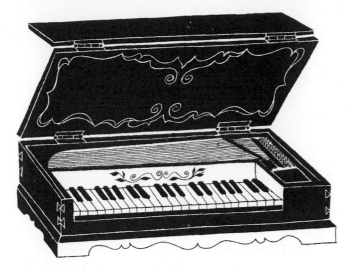

clavier (clah-veer') (FR. clah-v'yay), also **klavier** (GER. clah-veer')
1. The keyboard of such instruments as the piano, organ, etc.
2. Keyboard stringed instruments such as harpsichord, clavichord, piano, etc.

clef Fixes the pitch to the lines and spaces of the staff.
1. Fixed clefs:

G clef (treble) ⎰ sets the G above middle C.

F clef (bass) ⎰ sets the F below middle C.

2. Movable clef. The C clef sets middle C, and can be used any place on the staff:

The most commonly used today are:

C clef (alto) ⎰ used by the viola.

C clef (tenor) ⎰ used by trombone and cello.

The C clef is used to avoid writing leger lines above and below the staff.

coda (IT. co'da) A passage added to the final section of a piece or movement, to give the feeling of a definite ending; from the Italian word meaning "tail."
codetta (IT. coe-det'ta) Short coda. See **coda**.

col (IT. coal)
colla (IT. coal'lah) With the. *Col basso* means "with the bass."
coloratura (IT. coh-loh-rah-too'rah)
1. Brilliant vocal runs, containing many musical ornaments.
2. A voice capable of singing this kind of music.
combo (slang for "combination") A small group of musicians playing jazz. See **jazz**.
commodo (IT. co'moh-doh)
comodo (IT. co'moh-doh) Leisurely, comfortably.
common chord Major or minor chord. See **triad**.
compass The range of a voice or instrument.
con (IT. cone) With.
con amore (IT. ah-moh'ray) With love.

con anima (IT. ah'nee-mah) With soul, emotion; from the Italian word *anima*, meaning "soul." Composers have often used this term incorrectly to mean "with animation, lively."
con brio (IT. bree'oh) With spirit.
con calma (IT. cahl'mah) Calmly, serenely.
concert A public musical performance.
concertina An accordion-like, free-reed instrument with expandable bellows. The concertina is six-sided, with buttons at each end for playing melody and accompaniment. See **accordion**.

concertino See **concerto grosso.**

concerto (IT. cohn-chair'toh) An instrumental composition for solo performer accompanied by an orchestra. Concerto comes from the Latin *concertare,* meaning "to strive side by side." A concerto is usually in three movements.
See **concerto grosso, sonata form.**

concerto grosso (IT. cohn-chair'toe gro'soh) A work in concerto form for a small group of solo instruments and orchestra (as compared with the concerto—a work for a single solo instrument and orchestra). The concerto grosso form was most popular in the late seventeenth and eighteenth centuries. See **concerto.**

conductor Leader of the orchestra.
This is how the conductor indicates the beat to the orchestra.

2/4 time

3/4 time

4/4 time

contrabass (also called string bass, double bass, bass viol). A stringed instrument played with a bow; the largest and lowest-pitched of the string family. The contrabass has characteristics of both the violin and the viol families. Its four strings are tuned:

and sound an octave lower than written.
See **viol, violin.**

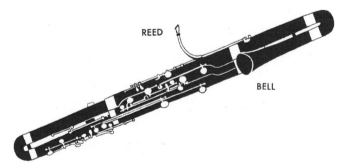

contrabassoon (also called double bassoon) A member of the oboe family. The contrabassoon has the deepest voice in the orchestra. It has a tube of over 16 feet in length, doubled on itself four times. The metal bell points downward, unlike the bassoon bell, which points upward. The contrabassoon performs best at slow or moderate speeds. See **bassoon.**

The contrabassoon range is written:

con forza (IT. for'tsah) With force.

con fuoco (IT. fwo'coh) With spirit, fire.

con furia (IT. foo'ree-ah) With fury; wildly.

con gioco (IT. joh'coh) Playfully, merrily.

con passione (IT. pahs-see-oh'nay) With passion, great emotion.

con slancio (IT. zlan'choh) With dash, vehemence; impetuously.

consonance The consonant intervals are: thirds, fourths, fifths, sixths and octaves. Consonance gives a feeling of satisfaction or rest, the opposite of dissonance. See **dissonance.**

con spirito (IT. spee'ree-toh) With vigor, spirit.

This is the actual sound:

contradanza (IT. cohn-trah-dahn′dsa)
contredanse (FR. cohn-tre-dahns) A dance popular in France at the close of the eighteenth century; probably came from the English country dance.
contralto (IT. cohn-trahl′toh) Lowest female voice; also called alto. See **alto 1.**
This is the range of the contralto voice:

contrapuntal (cahn-tra-pun′tal) Relating to counterpoint. See **counterpoint, polphony.**
contrary motion The voices of a composition moving in opposite directions.
cor anglais (FR. cawr ong-glay) English horn. See **English horn.**
coranto (IT. coh-rahn′toh)
corrente (IT. coh-ren′tay)
courante (FR. coo-rahnt) A dance that originated in the sixteenth century and later became part of the suite. See **suite 1.**

There are two distinct type of courante:
1. The Italian coranto (or corrente) is a rapid, constantly moving dance in triple time (three beats to the measure). It is usually in simple two-part (binary) form.
2. The French courante is also in triple time and binary form, but with six beats in the last measure of each section. It is slower and more elegant than the Italian coranto.

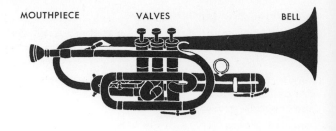

MOUTHPIECE   VALVES   BELL

cornet A brass wind instrument with valves, pitched in B flat. The cornet has a gradually expanding conical bore and a cup mouthpiece deeper than that of the trumpet. It is used in both military and brass bands. Its tone is mellower and less brilliant than that of the trumpet. See **trumpet, bore.**
The B flat cornet is a transposing instrument.

This is its written range: This is the actual sound:

See **transposing instruments.**

counterpoint Several independent but related melodies being played at the same time. The word "counterpoint" comes from the Latin *punctus contra punctum,* meaning "melody against melody."
See **polyphony.**

crescendo (IT. creh-shen′do) Growing louder. Abbreviation: *cresc.*
This is a crescendo sign: ———————

D

D Pitch name.
On the staff:

On the keyboard:

da capo (IT. dah cah'poh) From the beginning.
Abbreviation: *D. C.*
D. C. al fine means "go back to the beginning and play to *fine*."
D. C. al segno means "go back to the beginning and play to the sign."

dal segno (IT. dahl sane'yoh) From the sign: ·𝄋·
Abbreviation: *D. S.*
D. S. al fine means "go back to the sign and play to *fine*."

début (FR. day-bu) First public appearance.

decibel Unit for measuring loudness.
Abbreviation: db

décidé (FR. day-see-day) Definite, decided.

deciso (IT. day-chee'zoh) Bold, energetic, with decision.

decrescendo (IT. day-creh-shen'doh) Growing softer.
Abbreviation: *decresc.*
This is a decrescendo sign:

dehors (FR. deh-or) With emphasis, made to stand out.

delicato (IT. day-lee-cah'toh) In a refined and delicate manner.

cymbal Percussion instrument. One of two metal plates that produce clashing sounds of indefinite pitch when struck together. Cymbals may be used in pairs, or a single cymbal may be hung from a stand. Different ways of playing produce various effects. A continuing sound is made by rolling on the edge of the cymbal with drum-sticks. A crash can be made on a single cymbal by striking its edge.
The high-hat cymbals, a pair of cymbals on a stand operated by a foot pedal, are an important part of dance band percussion. See **tam-tam.**

czardas (HUNG. char'dahsh) A Hungarian national dance. The czardas usually has a slow, sad introduction called *lassu,* followed by a rapid, wild dance called *friss,* or *friska.*

détaché (FR. day-tah-shay) Detached.
development See **sonata form** 2.

diatonic (dy-a-ton'ic)
1. Referring to the tones of the major or minor scales.
2. A diatonic half step is a progression to a neighbor note, both notes having different letter names:

while a chromatic half step (which sounds the same as the diatonic), is a progression to the same note altered by an accidental, both notes having the same letter name:

diminished See **interval.**

diminuendo (IT. dee-mee-noo-en'doh) Growing softer.
Abbreviations: *dim., dimin.*
This is a diminuendo sign:

dissonance A discord. An interval or chord which is restless, requiring movement to a restful (or consonant) interval or chord. This movement from dissonance to consonance is called resolution. Dissonant intervals are: seconds, sevenths, and all augmented and diminished chords. See **consonance.**

divertimento (IT. dee-vare-tee-men'to) An instrumental form similar to both the suite and symphony, usually containing both dances and short movements, and played by a small group.

divisi (IT. dee-vee'zee) Divided. Used in instrumental music to indicate that chords are to be divided between the players. Abbreviations: div. (sometimes a2.)

dolce (IT. dohl'chay) Sweet, soft.

dolente (IT. doh-len'tay) Sad, doleful.

doloroso (IT. doh-loh-roh'soh) Sad, doleful.

dominant The fifth step of the major or minor scale. The dominant chord is a triad built on this tone.

dot
1. A dot after a note lengthens it by one half its value, thus in 4/4 time:

♩ = one beat

♩. = one and one half beats (same as ♩ ♪)

♩ = two beats

♩. = three beats (same as ♩ ♩)

2. A dot under or above a note means to play staccato. See **staccato, portamento.**

double bar

1. DOUBLE BAR   Appears at the end of a section.

2.   Appears at the end of a movement or piece.

double bass See **contrabass.**

double bassoon See **contrabassoon.**

double flat ♭♭ A double flat placed before a note lowers the note a whole step.

doucement (FR. doos-mah[n]) Sweetly.

downbeat The first beat of a measure, usually accented. In conducting, the downbeat is given with a downward motion of the hand.

drone
1. Name for those pipes of the bagpipe that continuously sound one tone each. See **bagpipe.**
2. Continuous and repetitious bass, similar to the drone of a bagpipe; called a drone bass. See **musette** 2.

drum A percussion instrument.
1. Snare drum. A small drum, with snares of gut or wire stretched across its lower head, that produces a dry, rattling tone. The snare drum consists of a wooden or metal shell, and two drum-heads which are tightened by rods attached to the shell. It is possible to release the snares to produce a hollow, tom-tom sound. It is played with a pair of wooden sticks. The snare drum is used in orchestras as well as in bands. See **roll.**

2. Tenor drum. Larger than the snare drum (see above). The tenor drum is constructed without snares. It is generally used in drum corps and played with felt-headed sticks. See **roll.**

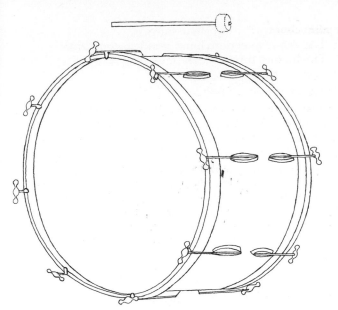

3. Bass drum. Largest of the drums. The bass drum consists of a large wooden shell and two drum-heads. The bass drum sounds no definite pitch. It is played with a stick having a knob of lamb's wool or of felt. A double-ended stick is used to produce roll effects. See **roll.**

4. Timpani (kettledrum). A metal kettle across which a drum-head is stretched. The kettledrum is the only drum that is tuned to an exact pitch. This is done by loosening or tightening the head, either with screws or a pedal. It is played with drumsticks having padded felt ends. Single notes or rolls may be sounded on the kettledrum. See **roll.**

duet   A composition for two performers.

dulcimer   An early stringed instrument played with two small hammers. The dulcimer consists of a wooden sound box across which the strings are stretched.

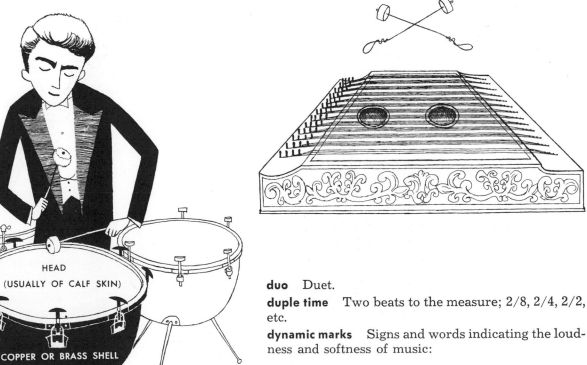

SCREWS

HEAD
(USUALLY OF CALF SKIN)

COPPER OR BRASS SHELL

duo   Duet.

duple time   Two beats to the measure; 2/8, 2/4, 2/2, etc.

dynamic marks   Signs and words indicating the loudness and softness of music:

crescendo: ————

decrescendo: ————

p f etc.

E

E Pitch name.

On the staff:

On the keyboard:

écossaise (FR. ay-coh-sez) A Scottish dance. The écossaise was originally accompanied by bagpipes, and was in 3/2 or 2/4 time. Later it developed into a country dance in rapid 2/4 time. It contains two four-measure or eight-measure sections with repeats.

Leggiero e animato   Ludwig van Beethoven (b. 1770)

"ECOSSAISE"

egualmente (IT. ay-gwahl-men'tay) Evenly, equally.

eighth See **octave**.

eighth note ♪ Eight of these equal one whole note. Two are equal to a quarter note.

eighth rest ℽ Measured silence equal to an eighth note.

elegy A sad and mournful composition; sometimes a musical setting for a sad poem.

Lento   Jules Massenet (b. 1842)

"ELEGIE"

embellishment A musical ornament. See **ornaments**.

embouchure (FR. ahn-bou-shure)
1. The mouthpiece of most wind instruments.
2. The lip and tongue technique used in playing these instruments.

energico (IT. ay-nare'gee-coh) With energy, vigor.

English horn An alto oboe; double-reed woodwind instrument. The English horn has a longer tube than the oboe, and has a pear-shaped bell. The metal tube that holds the reed is bent back at an angle. The instrument is neither English, nor is it a horn. Its tone is nasal and sad. The English horn is a transposing instrument.

This is the written range:

This is the actual sound:

See **transposing instruments.**

REED

PEAR-SHAPED BELL

ensemble (FR. ahn-sahnbl) The co-operation of several performers; (in contrast to solo music—for one performer only); from the French word meaning "together." See **chamber music.**

espressivo (IT. es-pres-see'voh) With expression and feeling. Abbreviation: *espress.*

étude (FR. ay-tewd) A piece to aid the technique of the student in the performance of his instrument; from the French word meaning "study."

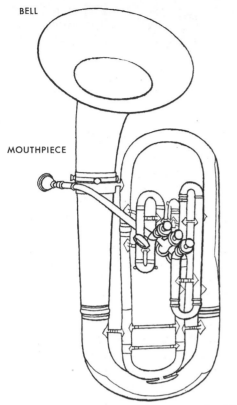

BELL

MOUTHPIECE

euphonium (u-fo'nee-um) A low-pitched brass wind instrument having a cup mouthpiece and valves. In the United States the name is used for the baritone. It is actually a small bore B flat bass tuba. The American euphonium is often constructed with two bells, one of which produces a trombone-like tone, the other a true baritone sound. In England the euphonium is made with a larger bore than the baritone, and is considered the highest in pitch of the tuba family.

When music is written for it in the bass clef it is non-transposing. When written in the treble clef, the parts are an octave and a tone above the actual pitch. When in the bass clef the range is written and sounds:

See **bore**.

evensong Evening prayer of the Anglican Church; vespers in the Roman Catholic Church.

exercise A technical study.

C. Czerny

Allegro

mf

"50 LITTLE STUDIES" VOLUME I, PART I

exposition See **sonata form** 1.

expression Expressing emotion through musical performance by varying dynamics (*forte* and *piano*), and speed (*accelerando, ritardando, rubato,* etc.).

F

F Pitch name.
On the staff:
On the keyboard:

𝆑 Loud. Abbreviation for *forte*.

facile (IT. fah'chee-lay) Easy, fluent.

falsetto (IT. fahl-set'toh) A false tone above the normal range of the voice. See **yodel**.

fandango (SPAN.) A lively Spanish dance in triple time (three beats to the measure). The fandango is danced by a single couple to the accompaniment of a guitar, castanets, and singing. It first appeared in Spain in the eighteenth century.

This is a typical fandango rhythm:

fanfare A flourish of trumpets.

fantaisie (FR. fahn-teh-zee)
fantasia (IT. fahn-tay'zee-ah)
fantasy (fan'ta-see)
1. A seventeenth- and eighteenth-century form based on free imitation of the voices.
2. Music in which the composer writes according to impulse, not following the strict forms of composition.

f clef Bass clef:  F
See **clef** 1.

fermata (IT. fair-mah'tah) ⌒ A hold or pause. The fermata increases the time value of the note or rest over which it is placed. The performer decides how long it shall be held.

feroce (IT. fair-oh'chay) Wild, fierce, ferocious.

fiddle A slang term for violin; also used for any other member of the string family, such as "bass fiddle."

fife A small flute-like instrument. The fife sounds an octave higher than the flute. It has from six to eight finger holes and no keys. It is used mainly in fife and drum corps.

fifth
1. The interval of five diatonic tones. See **interval**. From C up to G is a fifth:

From C down to F is a fifth:

2. The fifth step in a diatonic scale; the dominant.

figure Motive; shortest musical idea.

finale (IT. fee-nah'lay) Closing or final part or movement of a musical composition.

fine (IT. fee'nay) End, close. *D.C. al fine* means "go back to the beginning and play to *fine*."

flageolet (flaj-o-let')
1. A small flute-like instrument of the whistle family.
2. A high-pitched flute-stop on the organ.

flamenco (SP. flah-men'co) Name given to the gypsy style of Spanish song and dance. This style probably originated in the early nineteenth century from the *cante hondo,* an emotional and tragic type of Andalusian song. Toward the end of the nineteenth century it became more popular and colorful, the name "flamenco" possibly being used to describe the flamingo-colored garments worn by the gypsies. The song usually starts with "*Ay*" or "*Leli*," has a range of a sixth, and is usually accompanied by the guitar.

flat ♭ A flat placed before a note lowers the note by one chromatic half step. See **chromatic.**

fling A Scottish dance. The fling resembles the reel; it is usually in 4/4 time. See **reel.**

flute A woodwind instrument. The flute has a cylindrical tube. The tone is produced by blowing across the embouchure (the opening on the side of the mouthpiece joint). This joint, strangely enough, is conical rather than cylindrical, narrowing toward its tip. The key mechanism, placement of tone holes and system of fingering of the modern flute, were invented by Theobald Boehm (born about 1793). Although considered woodwinds, modern flutes are often made of metal. The tone of the flute is silvery and clear, becoming penetrating on the high notes. The flute is a non-transposing instrument (the music sounds exactly where written).

This is the range:

folk music Music that expresses the customs, traditions, and emotions of the people of a country or community. Folk music is not formally composed, but rather develops among the people.

Among the American folk songs are the mountain tunes, cowboy songs, and Negro spirituals:

Mountain tune:

From the val - ley they say you are go - ing,— We will

miss your bright eyes and sweet smile.

Cowboy song:

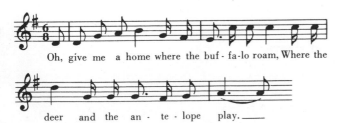

Oh, give me a home where the buf - fa - lo roam, Where the

deer and the an - te - lope play.—

Negro spiritual:

No - bo - dy knows the trou - ble I see,

No - bo - dy knows my sor - row,

form The pattern of a composition; the way in which the themes and development material are arranged. There are seven kinds of form in common use:

1. Simple binary—two-section form. See **binary.**
2. Simple ternary—three-section form. See **ternary.**
3. Compound binary—also called sonata form. See **sonata form.**
4. Rondo—see **rondo.**
5. Theme and variations—see **variation.**
6. Fugue—see **fugue.**
7. Single continuous form, without repeats or development. For example, the first prelude from J. S. Bach's "The Well Tempered Clavier." It is also possible to combine any of these forms in different ways.

forte (IT. for'tay) Loud. Abbreviation: f

forzando (IT. for-tsahn'doh)
forzato (IT. for-tsah'toh) With sudden stress or emphasis; forced, accented. Same as *sforzando*. Abbreviation: *fz*

These are the signs:

fourth
1. The interval of four diatonic tones. See **interval**. From C up to F is a fourth:

From C down to G is a fourth:

2. The fourth step in a diatonic scale; the subdominant.

free-reed See **reed** 3.

French horn A brass wind instrument. The French horn has a conical bore, a funnel-shaped mouthpiece, and a wide, flaring bell. The valves (which were added to the earlier natural horn) allow the horn to play a complete chromatic scale over its wide range. It has a mellow, majestic tone – penetrating in the high notes, rather brassy in the middle of the range. The extreme high and low notes are difficult to play.

MOUTHPIECE

VALVES

BELL

The French horn is built in F, B flat, or a combination of both (called double horn). The French horn is a transposing instrument.

This is its written range:

The horn in F sounds:

See **transposing instruments, bore**.

frets Narrow, raised lines crossing the finger board of the banjo, guitar, lute, mandolin, zither, etc. The frets show the proper placement of the fingers to produce the different pitches.

fugue (fewg) The most highly developed type of contrapuntal composition; from the Latin word *fuga,* meaning "flight." The fugue starts with a melody called the subject, which is stated at the beginning by one voice (melody) and is alternated with an answer that resembles the subject, but starts on a different tone (usually the fifth or fourth tone of the key). The subject is taken up alternately by each voice; there are usually two to five voices. Episodes are sections that do not contain the subject. If the subject overlaps in two or more voices, it is known as a stretto passage.
This is a portion of a Bach fugue:

subject

subject

subject

subject

fundamental
1. The root of a chord; the tone upon which a chord is built.
2. The first harmonic in the overtone series.
See **overtone series**.

furioso (IT. foo-ree-oh'soh) Wildly, furiously.

G

G Pitch name.
On the staff: On the keyboard:

gagliarda (IT. gahl-yar'dah)
galliard (gal-yard') A gay dance, usually in rapid triple time (three beats to a measure). The galliard was popular from the sixteenth to the middle of the seventeenth centuries. It was often performed following the pavane (a slower, statelier dance).
See **pavane.**

gavotte (FR. gah-voht) A seventeenth-century French dance in two-part form. Each phrase and section usually starts on the second half of the measure. The gavotte is frequently found as a movement of the suite. See **suite** 1.

g clef Treble clef: See **clef** 1.

gigue (FR. jheeg) Also called jig. An early Italian dance, which may have been named after the *giga*, a type of viol. The gigue was written in various meters: 3/8, 6/8, 12/8, 6/4. It was often used as the last movement of the eighteenth-century suite. See **suite** 1.

giocoso (IT. joh-coh'soh) Playful, merry.

glissando (IT. glees-sahn'doh) A rapid succession of notes. The glissando is played on a keyboard instrument by sliding a finger over the keys; on stringed instruments, by sliding a finger along the string while bowing. A glissando may also be played on some of the wind instruments. It is often found in harp music, where it is played by running a finger across the strings. Abbreviation: *gliss.*

glockenspiel (GER. glok'en-shpeel) Percussion instrument.
1. A set of tuned steel bars arranged like the keyboard of a piano; played with two wooden hammers.
2. Bell lyre—a portable glockenspiel.

gondoliera (IT. gohn-dol-yair'ah) A barcarole. See **barcarole.**

gong See **tam-tam.**

grace note See **appoggiatura** 2.

grandioso (IT. grahn-dee-oh'soh) Grand, bold.

grave (IT. grah'vay; FR. grahv) Slow, serious; slower than lento, faster than largo.

grazioso (IT. grah-tse-oh'soh) Graceful.

Gregorian chant Liturgical chant of the Roman Catholic Church, which was revised by Pope Gregory I (Pope from 590 to 604).

ground bass See **basso ostinato.**

guiro (CUBAN gwee'roh) Percussion instrument used in Latin American music. The guiro is a dried gourd with a notched top. The sound is produced by scraping the notches with a stick.

guitar A stringed instrument, played with a plectrum. The six-string guitar has a flat back and top, and a fretted finger board. It is now often equipped with microphone pickups and an amplifier.

J. C. F. Fischer (b. 1650?)

"GIGUE," "MELPOMENE" SUITE

PEGS
FRETS
STRINGS

H

habanera (SP. ah-bah-nair′ah) A slow Cuban dance that became popular in Spain. The habanera may have originated in Africa. The short introduction is followed by two sections of from eight to sixteen measures.

This is part of an habanera:

Sebastián Yradier (b. 1809)

"LA PALOMA"

half note ♩ Two of these equal one whole note. There are two quarter notes in one half note.

half rest ▬ A measured silence equal to a half note.

half step See **step** 2.

hammerklavier (GER. hahm-mer-clah-veer′) An old German name for pianoforte. The Beethoven Sonata Op. 106 is usually called the "Hammerklavier Sonata."

harmonica See **mouth organ**.

harmonic minor scale See **minor scale** 2.

harmonics
1. On a stringed instrument, harmonics are produced by placing the finger lightly on the string to divide it into halves, quarters, etc., so that all sections of the string then sound the same tone at the same time, a higher tone than if the finger pressed the string down to the finger board.
2. See **overtone series**.

harmony
1. A combination of tones sounding together; a chord.
2. The relationship between a series of chords; the chord structure of a musical composition.

harp A stringed instrument. The tone is produced by plucking the strings with the fingers. There are usually forty-seven strings and seven foot pedals, each pedal controlling a different set of strings. One pedal controls the C strings, one the D strings, etc. The harp is one of the oldest instruments. It is mentioned as early as 3000 B.C.

horn See **French horn.**

hornpipe An old English country dance of lively character. The hornpipe was popular from the sixteenth to the nineteenth centuries, and often was danced by sailors. Hornpipes of the seventeenth and eighteenth centuries were usually in 3/2 time, later in 4/4 time.

hunting horn Brass wind instrument. A simple coiled tube without valves. The hunting horn is a forerunner of the French horn. It was used in the hunt, carried over the performer's shoulder. It is a type of natural horn. See **French horn.**

harpsichord A forerunner of the piano. The strings are plucked by quills when the keys are pressed down (in contrast to the strings of the piano, which are struck by hammers). It is not possible to produce a crescendo or diminuendo on the harpsichord. However, it often has two keyboards, one producing loud tones, the other, soft. Stops or couplers are used to connect several sets of strings so that several octaves may be played by pressing down one key. The harpsichord was popular from the sixteenth to the eighteenth centuries. See **spinet, virginal(s).**

hold Pause. See **fermata.**

hopak (RUS. ho'pahk) also called **gopak** (RUS. go'-pahk) A lively Russian dance in duple time (two beats to the measure).

hymn A religious or sacred song.

John B. Dykes

Ho - ly, ho - ly, ho - ly, Lord God Al - might - y!

I

impromptu A piece written in a free, casual form; popular in the romantic period (nineteenth century). Impromptus often give the impression of being improvised; that is, composed as they are being played.

improvisation The art of composing music while performing it, without the aid of written music.

incalzando (IT. een-cahl-tsahn'doh) Hurrying.

incidental music Provides the background to a play. The Greek dramas frequently contained incidental music, as did the Shakespearean plays. Many modern plays use incidental music.

indeciso (IT. een-day-chee'soh) Undecided, hesitating.

inquieto (IT. een-kwee-ay'toh) Uneasy.

interval The difference in pitch between two tones. The standard diatonic intervals are:

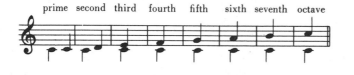

These diatonic intervals may be major or minor:

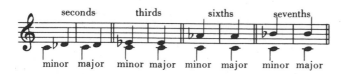

These diatonic intervals are perfect:

Diatonic intervals may be diminished or augmented:

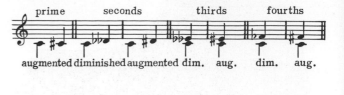

Diatonic intervals may be inverted. A major interval becomes minor when inverted, and vice versa. A perfect interval stays perfect when inverted.
See **inversion.**

intonation Having to do with playing or singing the correct pitch.

invention Title used by J. S. Bach for his two-part and three-part inventions (short pieces written in a free, contrapuntal style).

inversion

1. An interval is inverted when the lower note is placed an octave higher:

2. A chord is inverted when any note other than the root is the lowest note of the chord:

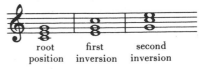

irresoluto (IT. eer-reh-zo-loo'toh) Undecided, hesitating.

J

jam session An informal get-together of musicians to play jazz without written music. See **improvisation, jazz.**

jazz Jazz in its various forms (starting with ragtime, and constantly developing harmonically and rhythmically through the blues, boogie-woogie, swing and bebop) has formed the basis for American dance music since the late 1890's when Negro street musicians in New Orleans adapted their African rhythms and melodies to a new style.

1. Ragtime was probably the earliest of the jazz forms. The harmonies are simple, using the I, IV, and V^7 chords. The rhythms are based on two or four to the bar, and were played in a very strict style. As most of the players did not read music, they had to improvise their parts.

2. The blues, which became popular around 1912, were originally vocal pieces. The tempo is slower than ragtime, and the harmonies are more complicated with a greater use of seventh chords. The break (a short improvised cadenza) is often used.

3. Boogie-woogie began in the 1920's. Its main feature is a repeated bass figure of steady eighth notes in 4/4 time, with free improvisation in the melody.

4. Swing developed out of the earlier forms. It has a greater harmonic vocabulary, using seventh and

ninth chords. The rhythm is based on two or four beats to the bar, but with a smooth, triplet feeling rather than the strict rhythms of the earlier jazz forms. Improvisation, breaks, etc., of the earlier forms are all used.

5. Bebop is a further development, both rhythmically and harmonically. The harmonies are very complicated, using sevenths, ninths, elevenths, and thirteenths, as well as all kinds of melodic and harmonic alterations. The rhythm is strict, with a feeling of sixteenth notes in a four-beat measure.

jig See **gigue.**

jota (SPAN. hoh'tah) A Spanish dance in triple time (three beats to the measure), danced by couples. The jota originated in Aragon (northern Spain). It is a rapid dance accompanied by castanets.

K

kettledrum Also called timpani. See **drum** 4.

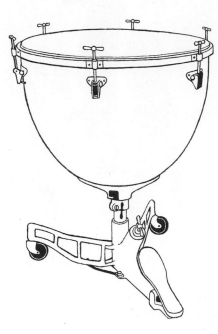

key
1. A key is major or minor, depending on whether it is based on the major or minor scale. Compositions written in a given key can use any note outside the scale as an accidental.
2. Key note. The first note of a scale; the tonic. See **tonic.**
3. Key signature. The sharps or flats following the clef at the beginning of each staff, which indicate the key or scale in which the piece is written.
4. One of a set of levers pressed by the fingers in playing the piano, or any other keyboard instrument.

5. The mechanism by which some of the tone holes are opened and closed on a wind instrument.

key note The tonic. See **key** 2.
key signature See **key** 3.
klavier (GER. clah-veer') See **clavier.**

L

lagrimoso (IT. lah-gree-moh'soh) Tearful.
lamento (IT. lah-men'toh) A sad, mournful piece.
lamentoso (IT. lah-men-toh'soh) Sorrowfully.

ländler (GER. lent'ler) A dance popular in Austria in the early nineteenth century; a kind of slow waltz.

Franz Schubert (b. 1797)

"LÄNDLER"

langsam (GER. lahn[k]'zahm) Slow.

largando (IT. lar-gahn'doh) Growing slower, broader; same as allargando.

larghetto (IT. lar-get'toh) Slow; faster than largo, slower than lento.

largo (IT. lar'goh) Broad, dignified; slowest tempo mark.

lead To conduct.
leader Conductor.
leading tone The seventh tone of the major and harmonic minor scales. It is called leading tone because it leads up one half step to the key note, or tonic.

legato (IT. lay-gah'toh) Connected, smooth. A slur is often used to indicate legato passages:

Abbreviation: *leg.*

ledger line
leger line Lines added above or below the staff to extend it for notes that are too high or too low to be written on the staff:

léger (FR. lay-jhay) Light.

leggermente (IT. led-jair-men'tay)
leggiermente (IT. led-jair-men'tay)
leggeramente (IT. led-jair-ah-men'tay) Lightly, swiftly.

leggero (IT. led-jair'oh)
leggiero (IT. led-jair'oh) Light, swift, airy. Abbreviation: *legg.*

lentamente (IT. len-tah-men'tay) Slowly.

lento (IT. len'toh) Slow; faster than largo, slower than andante.

L.H. Left hand.

libretto (IT. lee-bret'toh) The words or text of an opera, oratorio, etc.; from the Italian word meaning "little book."

lied (GER. leedt) Song.

l'istesso (IT. lees-stess'oh) The same.

loco (IT. loh'coh) Place. Used after *8va* to show that the notes are to be played in their normal "place."

lontano (IT. lohn-tah'noh) Distant.

loure (FR. loor)
1. Sixteenth-century French name for bagpipe. See **bagpipe.**
2. French seventeenth-century dance in moderate 6/4 time, possibly accompanied by the loure (see 1, above).

"LOURE," FRENCH SUITE NO. 5

lute A stringed instrument most popular during the sixteenth and seventeenth centuries. The lute is played by plucking the strings (which are strung in pairs). It is pear-shaped, and has a flat neck with seven or more frets. The pegbox is bent back at an angle to help withstand the pull of the strings.

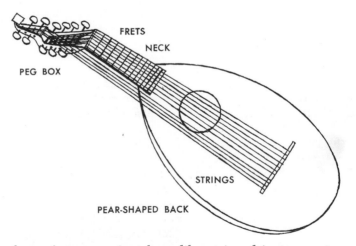

lyre A very ancient harp-like stringed instrument. It has had many names and shapes in its long history, but generally consists of a sound box, two arms, and a yoke (or crossbar). In its many forms the strings have either been plucked with the fingers, struck with a plectrum, or, in some kinds of lyre, bowed. The earliest known examples were found in the royal tombs of Ur.

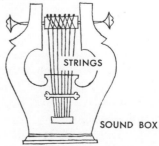

M

ma (IT. mah) But. *Allegro ma non troppo* means "fast, but not too much so."

madrigal Unaccompanied secular (non-religious) choral music in contrapuntal style, popular from the fourteenth to the seventeenth centuries. Madrigals were usually sung with one voice to a part.

maestoso (IT. mah-es-toe'soh) Dignified, majestic.

major scale A diatonic scale containing five whole steps and two half steps in the following pattern:

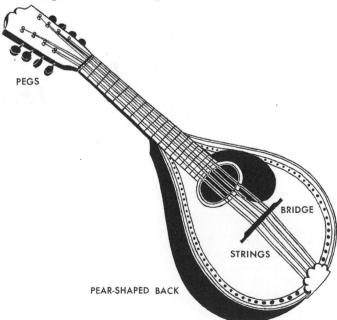

See **tetrachord.**

mambo (mahm'bo) A Latin American dance that first appeared in the early 1950's.

mancando (IT. mahn-cahn'doh) Dying away, growing softer.

mandolin The only instrument of the lute family in common use today. The mandolin has a pear-shaped body. The strings, which are in four pairs, are played with a plectrum. The finger board is fretted.

PEGS

BRIDGE

STRINGS

PEAR-SHAPED BACK

maraca (CUBAN mah-rah'cah) Percussion instrument used for rattle effect in Latin American music. The maraca is a dried gourd with beads or beans inside, and a handle so that it may be shaken. Maracas are used in pairs.

marcato (IT. mar-cah'toh) Accented, stressed, marked. Abbreviation: *marc.*

march Music for marching; usually in 4/4, 2/4, or 6/8 time.

marimba A percussion instrument. The marimba is a set of tuned wooden bars arranged like a piano keyboard, with a hollow tube (resonator) under each bar. It is played with mallets using different heads for different effects.

Originally from Africa, the marimba is popular today throughout the Americas. It is similar to the xylophone, but is pitched lower. Its range is about five octaves.

martellato (IT. mar-tel-ah'toh) Hammered.

Mass A solemn service of the Roman Catholic Church. The musical portion of the Mass usually consists of the Kyrie, Gloria in excelsis Deo, Credo, Sanctus, and Agnus Dei.

mazurka (POL. mah-zoor'cah) A Polish country dance from the province of Mazovia, Poland. The mazurka is usually in 3/8 or 3/4 time. It is generally written in two or four sections, each of which is repeated. There is a strong accent on the second or third beat.

M.D. Right hand. Abbreviation for *mano destra* (IT.), or *main droite* (FR.).

measure The notes or rests contained between two bar lines. The number of beats in the measure is shown by the time signature (see **time signature**). The first beat of each measure is usually slightly accented. The measure is frequently called the "bar."

mellophone An E-flat alto horn, member of the brass family. The mellophone has a conical bore, cup mouthpiece, and three valves. It is a transposing instrument.

This is its written range:

This is the actual sound:

See **transposing instruments, bore.**

melodic minor scale See **minor scale** 3.

melody Tune, air, theme.

meno (IT. may'noh) Less. *Meno mosso* means "less quickly" or "slower."

menuet See **minuet.**

menuett See **minuet.**

menuetto See **minuet.**

meter The regular grouping of beats and accents in a musical composition, indicated by the time signature.
1. Simple or common meter (time).
duple meter (two beats to a measure): 2/2, 2/4, 2/8.
triple meter (three beats to a measure): 3/2, 3/4, 3/8.
quadruple meter (four beats to a measure): 4/2, 4/4, 4/8.
2. Compound meter. The top figure of the time signature may be divided evenly by the number three:
compound duple: 6/2, 6/4, 6/8. (two or six beats to the measure)
compound triple: 9/2, 9/4, 9/8. (three or nine beats to the measure)
compound quadruple: 12/2, 12/4, 12/8. (four or twelve beats to the measure)
See **time signature.**

metronome A mechanical instrument that can be set to tick at various speeds. It is used to set the speed of musical compositions, also as an aid in keeping time. M.M. ♩ = 80, at the beginning of a piece or section, means that a quarter note equals one beat when the metronome is set at 80. There are then 80 clicks (or quarter notes) a minute. See **M.M.**

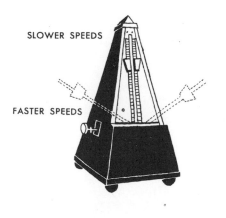

SLOWER SPEEDS

FASTER SPEEDS

mezzo (IT. med'zoh) Half. *Mezzo forte* means "half loud," or "medium loud."

mezzo-soprano The female voice with a range that lies between soprano and alto, and having some of the qualities of both.
This is the range of the mezzo-soprano:

M.G. Left hand. Abbreviation for *main gauche* (FR.).

military band Instrumental group made up of woodwind, brass, and percussion instruments. The military band was originally used to provide music for military purposes. The term has come to be used for bands using a similar instrumentation, such as school bands.

minor scale There are three types of minor scales:
1. Natural minor—contains the same notes as its relative major scale, but starts on the sixth step of the major scale:

The scale of D minor is related to the scale of F major, and has the same key signature. See **related keys.**
2. Harmonic minor—The seventh step of the natural minor scale is raised:

3. Melodic minor—The sixth and seventh steps of the natural minor are raised going up the scale, and return to the natural minor going down:

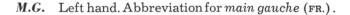

minuet (min-you-et′) An early French dance in 3/4 time and in moderate speed. The word "minuet" may have come from the French word *menu*, meaning "small," referring to the steps of the dance.

minuetto (IT. mee-noo-et′toh) See **minuet.**

misterioso (IT. mee-stay-ree-oh′soh) Mysterious.

M.M. Maelzel's metronome. See **metronome.**

modes Octave scales, dating back to the early Greeks, each with a different arrangement of half and whole steps, on which medieval church music was based. Our major and minor scales grew out of these church modes.

moderato (IT. mo-day-rah′toh)
1. In moderate speed; faster than andante, slower than allegretto.
2. Moderately; *allegro moderato* means "moderately fast."

modulation Going from one key to another within a composition.

molto (IT. mohl′toh) Very; *molto allegro* means "very fast."

morceau (FR. more-soh) A short musical composition.

mordent A musical ornament.

Mordent: is played:

When written ∿ it is now usually called "inverted mordent" and is played:

See **ornaments.**

morendo (IT. moh-ren′doh) Dying away; a gradual diminuendo, usually on a cadence or ending.

mosso (IT. mohs′soh) Moved; *più mosso* means "more moved," or quicker; *meno mosso* means "less moved," or slower.

motet A composition for voices in contrapuntal style, without accompaniment (a capella), usually for performance in church; from the French word *mot*, meaning "word."

motif (FR. moe-teef)

motive Figure, subject, or part of a theme.

moto (IT. moh′toh) Motion; *con moto* means "with motion," or quicker.

mouth organ (also called harmonica) A free-reed instrument played by the mouth. The mouth organ is a small box containing reeds, each with a separate opening for the wind, set into a metal plate.

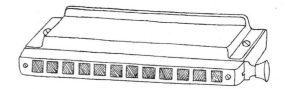

movement A section of a sonata, symphony, suite, concerto, etc., complete in itself, but forming, with other movements, a larger work.
See **sonata, symphony, suite, concerto,** etc.

musette (FR. meu-zet)
1. A small bagpipe. See **bagpipe.**
2. A piece imitating a bagpipe.
In this example the bass represents the drone of the bagpipe:

Allegro giocoso   Johann Sebastian Bach (b. 1685)

"MUSETTE"

N

natural ♮ The natural sign placed before a note that has been sharped or flatted, returns it to its original pitch.

natural minor scale See **minor scale** 1.

ninth The interval of nine diatonic tones. See **interval.**
This is a ninth:

nocturne (FR. nok-turn) Night piece; a dreamy, romantic piece popular in the 1800's. The nocturne usually has a broken-chord accompaniment. The first nocturnes were composed by John Field (1782-1837), from whom Chopin borrowed the idea and the title.

Frédéric Chopin (b. 1810)

"NOCTURNE" IN E♭

non (IT. nohn) Not; *Allegro ma non troppo* means "quick, but not too much so."

notation The signs and symbols used for written music.

O

obbligato (IT. ob-blee-gah'toh) An instrumental part accompanying, and nearly as important as, the solo part; from the Italian word meaning "necessary, obligatory."

oboe A woodwind instrument with a conical bore and double reed. The oboe has a rather piercing and nasal tone quality. See **wind instruments** 2, **bore.**
This is the range of the oboe:

REED

BELL

octave The interval of eight diatonic tones. See **interval.**
This is an octave:

opera A drama (either tragic or comic) usually entirely sung, with orchestral accompaniment, acting, scenery, and costumes.

operetta Light opera; opera in which there are some spoken parts. See **opera.**

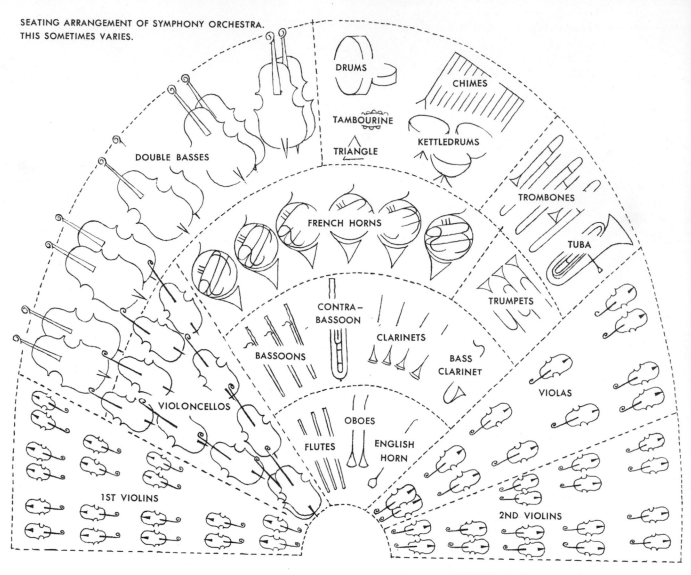

Labels in the orchestra diagram: DRUMS, CHIMES, TAMBOURINE, KETTLEDRUMS, TRIANGLE, DOUBLE BASSES, TROMBONES, FRENCH HORNS, TUBA, TRUMPETS, CONTRA-BASSOON, CLARINETS, BASSOONS, BASS CLARINET, VIOLAS, VIOLONCELLOS, OBOES, FLUTES, ENGLISH HORN, 1ST VIOLINS, 2ND VIOLINS

opus   A work. Abbreviation: op. or Op.
Most composers number their works in this manner:
Title, Op. 1, No. 1

oratorio   A fairly long, usually religious work for solo voices, chorus, and orchestra.

orchestra   A group of musicians performing on string, woodwind, brass, and percussion instruments. The modern symphony orchestra has about one hundred members, most of whom play stringed instruments.

organ   A keyboard wind instrument. The tone is produced by wind blown through pipes, each pipe sounding one tone. The organ has keyboards both for hands and feet. The keyboards played with the hands are called manuals; those played with the feet are called pedal keyboards; the different sets of pipes are controlled by buttons or levers called stops. Large organs having many sets of pipes (registers) produce a great variety of tone color. In the modern organ, the wind is supplied by electric bellows. In the older instruments, wind was pumped by foot pedals or by assistants who did the pumping.

organ point   See **pedal point**.

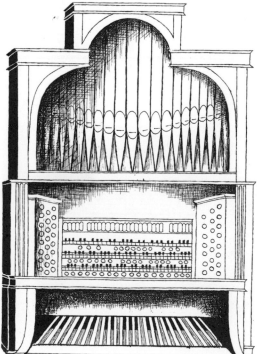

ornaments Musical embellishments such as: acciaccatura, appoggiatura, arpeggio, grace note, mordent, trill, turn, etc. Musical ornaments arose from the performers' desire to add to the written music. These ornaments are sometimes written out, but more often are replaced by signs. See **Table of Musical Signs.**

ossia (IT. o-see'ah) Alternate; another way to play a passage, usually easier.

ottava (IT. aw-tah'vah) Octave. *All' ottava (8va--------* or *8-------)* over the notes means to play an octave higher; below the notes, an octave lower.

overtone series All musical instruments produce tones which are made up of a fundamental (the main sound) and various harmonics (additional pure tones) above the fundamental. Because these harmonics or overtones are much softer than the fundamental, they are not heard distinctly. It is the overtone pattern which being similar in all instruments of the same kind, makes them all have a similar tone quality. Thus all clarinets have a clarinet quality. This is the overtone series built on the fundamental of C below the bass staff:

The black notes indicate notes in the series which are slightly out of tune.

overture Music usually serving as an introduction to a ballet, opera, or oratorio. However, the concert overture of the nineteenth century (such as Brahms' "Academic Festival Overture") is an independent piece, either in sonata form or in a free style. These overtures were usually inspired by an event, literary work, or program. See **program music, sonata form.**

P

p Soft. Abbreviation for *piano.*

P., Ped. Abbreviations for pedal.

panpipes A primitive wind instrument consisting of reed pipes of varying lengths bound together. The panpipes are played by blowing across the open end of the pipes.

partita (IT. par-tee'tah) A suite, set of pieces, or a series of variations. The partita was popular in the seventeenth and eighteenth centuries. See **suite.**

part song A choral composition for two or more voices in harmony.

passacaglia (IT. pahs-sah-cahl'yah)
passacaille (FR. pahs-sah-ky[ee])
See **chaconne** and **passacaglia.**

passage A portion or small section of a musical composition.

passepied (FR. pahss-p'yay) A gay, quick French dance, usually in 3/8 time, with the phrases beginning on the third beat.

passing note A note that does not belong to the harmony, but merely passes by step from one chord tone to the next.
The notes marked with a slanting line are passing notes:

"DIXIE"

41

passionato (IT. pahs-see-oh-nah'toh) With feeling, passion.

pastorale (IT. pass-toh-rah'lay; FR. pahs-tor-ahl)
1. A melody in 6/8, 9/8, or 12/8 time, imitating the instruments (shawms, pipes) and music of shepherds; usually with a flowing melody and drone bass.

2. A dramatic performance based on rustic, rural life; as performed in the late fifteenth century, the pastorale was a forerunner of the opera.

pause See **fermata**.

pavana (IT. pah-vah'nah)
pavane (FR. pah-vahn) A stately European court dance of the early sixteenth century. The pavane had slow, solemn movements, like those of a strutting peacock. The word "pavane" may have come from the Latin word *pavo*, meaning "peacock." The dance was usually in slow duple time (two beats to the measure), and was often performed with the galliard. See **galliard**.

pedal A mechanism of the piano, organ, harpsichord, or harp, worked by the feet.
1. Piano pedals control the dampers or the hammer position. See **piano**.
2. Organ pedals include the pedal keyboard as well as the volume pedal.
3. Harpsichord pedals control the tone quality by changing the kind of pick that plucks the strings (a soft pick produces a soft tone, while a hard pick produces a loud tone).
4. Harp pedals raise and lower the pitch of the strings to produce accidentals.
Abbreviations: 𝄢, 𝆏.

pedal point A long-held or continuously-repeated tone that may or may not be related to the harmonies of the other parts; also called organ point.

percussion family Instruments that are played by striking with a mallet or stick, by striking one against the other, or by shaking.
The percussion instruments are: bass drum, carillon, castanets, celesta, chimes, cymbals, glockenspiel, guiro, kettledrum (timpani), maracas, marimba, snare drum, tambourine, tam-tam (gong), triangle, xylophone, etc.

perdendo (IT. pare-den'doh)
perdendosi (IT. pare-den'doh-see)
Gradually dying away, growing softer.

period A small section of a composition, usually containing two phrases.

peu à peu (FR. pu[h] ah pu[h]) Little by little, gradually.

pesante (IT. pay-zahn'tay) Heavy.

phrase A complete musical thought. In the example the curved line above the notes is a phrase mark:

TWO-PART DANCE, THIRTEENTH CENTURY

piano (IT. pee-ah'noh) Soft. Abbreviation: *p*

piano A stringed keyboard instrument. It was called pianoforte because it produced both *piano* (soft) and *forte* (loud) tones. The strings are struck by hammers, which are connected to the keys through a complex mechanical device called the action. There are three pedals:
1. The *sostenuto* pedal, on the right (often mistakenly called the loud pedal), sustains or holds all tones played while it is down.
2. The *solo sostenuto*, the middle pedal, sustains or holds a single tone or chord.
3. The *una corda* pedal, on the left, the soft pedal, mutes or softens the tone.

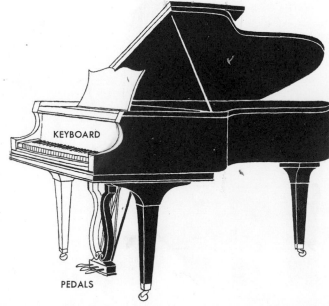

KEYBOARD

PEDALS

piccolo A small flute, pitched an octave higher than the concert flute. The piccolo has an extremely bright and penetrating tone. It sounds an octave higher than written.

This is the written range:

8va (8 notes higher)

pitch The exact location of a sound in the complete range of tones. This is governed by the number of vibrations per second (frequency) of the vibrating body (string, air column, etc.). For example, to sound the pitch of the A above middle C, any instrument must produce 440 vibrations per second.

più (IT. pew) More. *Più mosso* means "more movement," or faster.

pizzicato (IT. peet-see-cah'toh) To pluck, instead of bowing, the strings of a stringed instrument. Abbreviation: *pizz.*

placido (IT. plah'chee-doh) Placid, calm.

plectrum A small piece of metal, plastic, or some other material, used to pluck the strings of such instruments as the guitar, mandolin, ukulele, zither, etc.

poco (IT. poh'coh) Little. *Poco a poco* means "little by little," gradually.

polacca (IT. poh-lah'cah) A polonaise. See **polonaise.**

polka A lively round dance in 2/4 time. The polka appeared around 1830 in Bohemia, and became extremely popular in all of Europe. It remained a favorite until the close of the nineteenth century.
This is a typical polka rhythm:

polonaise A Polish dance in 3/4 time, of stately yet festive mood. The polonaise was originally performed for court processions and ceremonies. Frédéric Chopin made the dance a symbol of Polish nationalism.

"POLONAISE"

polyphonic (pol-i-fon'ic) See **polyphony.**

polyphony (poe-lif'o-nee) Music that consists of two or more independent voices (melodies) sounding together; also called counterpoint. The word polyphony comes from the Greek words meaning "many voices." See **counterpoint.**

pomposo (IT. pom-poh'soh) Majestic, dignified, pompous.

portamento (IT. por-tah-men'toh) In vocal, violin, and trombone music, portamento means to glide quickly from one tone to the next. In piano music, it is a half staccato, and is written:

prelude (preh'lood) A musical introduction. In the time of Johann Sebastian Bach (1685–1750), preludes were coupled with fugues, or were introductory pieces in the suite. With Frédéric Chopin (1810–1849) the prelude became an independent piece.

Molto agitato　　　　　　　　　　F. Chopin

"PRELUDE" OP. 28, NO. 22

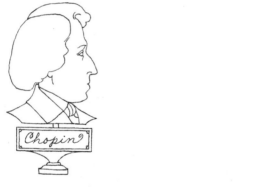

Chopin

prestissimo (IT. preh-stees'see-moh) As fast as possible.

presto (IT. pres'toh) Very fast; faster than allegro, slower than prestissimo.

prime
1. The root of a chord.
2. The first note of a scale (keynote).
3. The interval of a unison.

processional A hymn or organ solo performed in church during the processions of the choir and clergy.

program music Music designed to tell a story, portray a picture, illustrate an event, or create a mood; the opposite of absolute music (music composed with no such intentions; pure music). The earliest program pieces described horn calls, bird cries, bells, and battles. Rimsky-Korsakoff's symphonic suite, "Scheherazade," is an example of program music.

psaltery (sawl'ter-ee) An early stringed instrument similar to the dulcimer in construction, but plucked with the fingers or a plectrum rather than struck with hammers. See **dulcimer.**

pulse Beat, accent.

Q

quadrille (cwah-dril') A French dance of the early 1800's. The meter of the quadrille alternates between 6/8 and 2/4. The dance was performed by several couples, moving in a square. The themes were usually chosen from popular or operatic airs.

quadruple time Four beats to the measure: 4/8, 4/4, 4/2, etc.

quarter note ♩ Four of these equal one whole note. Two are equal to a half note.

quarter rest 𝄽 A measured silence equal to a quarter note.

quartet A composition for four instruments or voices. A string quartet is written for two violins, viola, and cello. See **chamber music.**

quasi (cwah'zee) Almost; as if. *Allegretto quasi allegro* means "lively, almost fast."

quintet A composition for five instruments or voices. See **chamber music.**

quintuple time Five beats to the measure: 5/8, 5/4, 5/2, etc.

R

ragtime   See **jazz** 1.

rallentando (IT. rah-len-tahn'doh) Gradually growing slower. Abbreviation: *rall.*

rapido (IT. rah'pee-doh) Quick, rapid.

recapitulation   See **sonata form** 3.

recessional   A hymn or organ solo performed in church as the choir and clergy leave after services.

recital   A public musical performance; a concert.

recitative (res-i-ta-teev') Vocal composition without fixed rhythm, imitating the sounds of speech. Recitative is used in opera, oratorio, etc., to carry on the story.

recorder   An end-blown flute with a whistle (fipple) mouthpiece. The recorder has a soft, gentle tone. It was popular in the sixteenth and seventeenth centuries, and was revived in the 1920's. It is still gaining in popularity. There are four kinds of recorder:
1. descant (soprano)
2. treble (alto)
3. tenor
4. bass

reed   A strip of cane or metal which, by vibrating, causes the air column to vibrate, thus producing the sound in many wind instruments:

MOUTHPIECE

REED

1. Clarinet family—single reed beating against the mouthpiece.
2. Oboe family—double reed, two sections beating against each other.
3. Mouth organ, accordion, concertina, etc.—separate metal reeds for each tone (also called free-reeds).

reed instrument   One whose sound is produced by the vibration of a reed. See **reed.**

reel   A dance performed by two or more couples moving in a circle. The reel is in rapid duple time (two beats to the measure), and contains four or eight measures that are constantly repeated. It is popular in Scotland, Ireland, and America.

register   The different sections in the range of voices and instruments.

related keys   Major and minor keys having the same signature. All major keys have a related minor, which starts on the sixth step of the major scale.
This is the key signature for both G major and E minor:

repeat   Play again.
These are the repeat signs found at the beginning and the close of the section to be repeated:

45

rest A sign indicating a measured silence.
See **whole rest, half rest, quarter rest, eighth rest, sixteenth rest, thirty-second rest, sixty-fourth rest.**

retenant (FR. re[h]-te[h]-nah[n]) Suddenly holding back the speed.

R.H. Right hand.

rhapsody A fantasy in free form, of heroic, national, or folk character. See **fantasy.**

rhumba See **rumba.**

rhythm Everything concerned with time or beat in music.

rigadoon

rigaudon (FR. ree-goh-doh[n]) A lively French dance of the seventeenth century. The rigaudon was originally a peasant dance that later became popular in the courts of Louis XIII, XIV, and XV. It was known as the rigadoon in England.

Edward MacDowell (b. 1861)
Allegro quasi allegretto

"RIGAUDON" OP. 49, NO. 2

rigore (IT. ree-go'ray) Strict, rigorous. *Con rigore* means "in strict time."

rinforzando (IT. reen-for-tsahn'doh) Emphasized, stressed, reinforced.
Abbreviations: *rf, rfz, rinf.*

risoluto (IT. ree-zo-loo'toh) Decided, definite, resolute.

ritardando (IT. ree-tar-dahn'doh) Gradually growing slower; rallentando. Abbreviations: *rit., ritard.*

ritenuto (IT. ree-ten-oo'toh) Suddenly slower; often incorrectly used in the same sense as rallentando or ritardando. Abbreviation: *riten.*

ritmico (IT. reet'mee-coh) Rhythmic.

roll A buzzing effect on the snare drum, produced by a rapid, alternating tap-bounce of the sticks in each hand. See **drum** 1.

Rolls are also produced on the timpani (kettledrum), using single strokes, and on the bass drum and cymbal as well.

romance

romanza (IT. roh-mahn'zah) A composition of romantic, tender songlike nature.

romantic A style of composition that developed in the nineteenth century, following the classical period. Romantic music emphasizes expression rather than form. Among the romantic composers are Schubert, Berlioz, Mendelssohn, Schumann, Chopin, Liszt, Brahms, and Wagner.

rondo A piece in which the main theme is alternated with contrasting themes. In the following example "A" stands for the main theme, the other letters stand for the contrasting themes: A b A c A
Rondos are usually gay, playful, and fast. They are often last movements of sonatas, concertos, and symphonies.

root The tone on which a chord or scale is built; the tonic. A triad is in the root position if the root is the lowest note.
This chord is built on C; C is the root:

Root position   1st inversion   2nd inversion

See **inversion** 2.

round A form of canon in which the voices enter at regular periods, on the same note repeating the same melody. A popular round is "Three Blind Mice."
See **canon.**

rubato (IT. roo-bah'toh) From the Italian word meaning "robbed"—robbing time from one part of a phrase (hurrying), and adding time to another part of the phrase (slowing).

rumba A Cuban dance, influenced by African rhythms. It became a popular dance form in the United States in the 1930's. A typical syncopated rumba rhythm is:

run A rapid, scale-like passage.

S

saltarello (IT. sahl-tah-rel'loh) An Italian dance of the sixteenth century; from *saltare,* meaning "to jump." The music is light and rapid, and in triple time (three beats to the measure). The saltarello was still popular in the nineteenth century, becoming a more violent dance. Saltarello was used as the name of a dance as early as the fourteenth century.

Nikolaus Ammerbach (1530-97)

"SALTARELLO"

samba A popular Latin-American dance form.

sans (FR. sah[n]) Without.

saraband
sarabanda (IT. sah-rah-bahn'dah)
sarabande (FR. sah-rah-bahnd) A stately dance of the sixteenth, seventeenth, and eighteenth centuries. The sarabande is in slow triple time (three beats to the measure), often with an accent or longer note on the second beat:

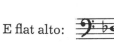

It is believed that the dance came from the Orient and was originally a wild love dance. The sarabande was brought to Spain in the early 1500's. Later it appeared in England and France as a slightly less violent dance. Finally it became the dignified dance often found in J. S. Bach's suites.

Sostenuto ed espressivo   Johann Sebastian Bach (b. 1685)

"SARABANDE" FRENCH SUITE NO. 6 (KEY OF E)

saxhorn A family of brass instruments having cup mouthpieces, a conical bore, and valves, introduced by Adolphe Sax about 1845. There were seven instruments ranging from deep bass to high treble. See **bore.**

saxophone A metal wind instrument with a single reed and a conical bore. It was invented by Adolphe Sax about 1840 in Belgium. It has a mellow, full tone.

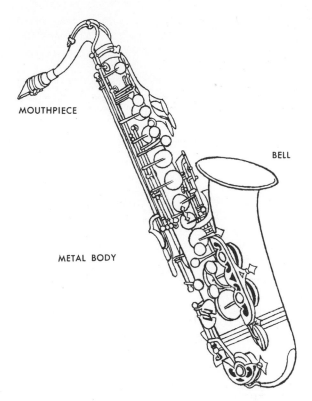

MOUTHPIECE

BELL

METAL BODY

All saxophones are transposing instruments and have the same written range:

but sound:

E flat alto:

B flat tenor:

E flat baritone:

B flat bass:

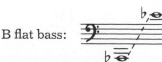

See **transposing instruments, bore.**

47

scale   A series of notes arranged in steps; from the Italian word *scala*, meaning "ladder." There are two main types of scales:
1. Diatonic scales:
   a. Major. See **major scale**.
   b. Minor. See **minor scale**.
See **diatonic, mode**.
2. Chromatic scale (see **chromatic** 1).

scherzando   (IT. scare-tsahn'doh) Playfully, jokingly.

scherzo   (IT. scare'tsoh) A joking, playful piece usually in rapid triple time (three beats to the measure);

Ludwig van Beethoven

"SONATA IN A" OP. 2 NO. 2

Beethoven used the scherzo in place of the traditional minuet in his symphonies and many of his sonatas. Chopin and Brahms composed several serious compositions entitled "Scherzo."

schnell   (GER. shnel) Quick.

schottische   (shot'tish) A round dance of the nineteenth century similar to a slow polka. It was known as the "German Polka" in England. The schottische is usually in duple time (two beats to the measure).

sec   (FR. sek) In a crisp style; the French word meaning "dry."

second   The diatonic interval between two neighboring notes.
Major second: Minor second:

(whole step)   (half step)

See **interval**.

segno   (IT. sane'yoh) Sign: 𝄋
al segno means "to the sign."
dal segno means "from the sign." Abbreviation: *D.S.*

seguidilla   (SP. say-ghee-dee'ya) A Spanish dance in triple time (three beats to the measure), often in a minor key. The seguidilla is usually accompanied by a guitar, voice, and castanets. This dance appears in the first act of the opera, *Carmen*, by Georges Bizet.

semitone   A half step. See **step** 2.

semplice   (IT. sem'plee-chay) Simple.

sempre   (IT. sem'pray) Always.

sentimento   (IT. sen-tee-men'toh) Feeling, sentiment.

senza   (IT. sen'tzah) Without.

sequence   The repetition of a melody (sometimes with slight variations), starting on a different pitch each time it is repeated.

Andante maestoso   G. F. Handel

motive   sequence   motive

"CHACONNE," "VARIATION I"

serenade
1. A romantic song; evening music.
2. An instrumental piece composed for a small group of string and wind instruments.

48

serio (IT. say'ree-oh) Serious.

serioso (IT. say-ree-oh'soh) In a serious style.

seventh   The interval of seven diatonic tones:

See **interval**.

seventh chord   A chord containing a root, third, fifth, and seventh. There are five kinds of seventh chords. Using C as the root, they are:

1. C⁷

2. C major⁷ (C chord with a major 7th)

3. C minor⁷

4. C augmented⁷

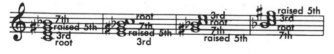

5. C diminished⁷ (The diminished seventh chord is built up in minor thirds. Any tone of the chord may be used as the root.)

sextet   A composition for six instruments or voices. See **chamber music**.

sforzato (IT. sfor-tsah'toh)

sforzando (IT. sfor-tsahn'doh) With sudden stress or emphasis; forced. Abbreviations: *sfz, sf*

These are the signs:

sharp ♯   A sharp placed before a note raises the note one chromatic half step. See **chromatic**.
F sharp on the staff: F sharp on the keyboard:

siciliano (IT. see-chee-l'ya'noh)

sicilienne (FR. see-seel-yen) A seventeenth- and eighteenth-century Sicilian dance in 6/8 or 12/8 time. The sicilienne usually has a flowing accompaniment of broken chords, with a lyrical melody. It often appears as a slow movement in early suites such as those by Corelli and J. S. Bach.

signature   See **key** 3, **time signature**.

simile (IT. see'mee-lay) Similar. To continue in a similar way; usually refers to a group of figures, phrases, etc., to be played in exactly the same way. Abbreviation: *sim.*

sixteenth note ♪   Sixteen of these equal one whole note; four are equal to a quarter note.

sixteenth rest ♪   A measured silence equal to a sixteenth note.

sixth   The interval of six diatonic tones:

See **interval**.

sixty-fourth note ♪   Sixty-four of these equal one whole note; four are equal to a sixteenth note.

sixty-fourth rest ♪   A measured silence equal to a sixty-fourth note.

skip   A melodic interval larger than a second:

See **interval**.

slentando (IT. zlen-tahn'doh) Growing slower.

slur  A curved line indicates:
1. that the notes are to be played legato (connected):

2. a phrase or a portion of a phrase. See **phrase**.
3. that when a note followed by another note of the same pitch is connected with a slur, it is a tie. The tie indicates that the second note is not to be played, but rather held for its full value:

4. that if the slur is placed above or below staccato dots, the notes are to be played slightly detached:

smorzando (IT. zmor-tsahn′doh) Dying away, fading. Abbreviation: *smorz.*

snare drum See **drum** 1.

solfeggio (IT. sole-fed′joh) Vocal exercises sung on the syllables *do, re, mi,* etc., using C as the fixed *do.*

solo Alone. A solo piece is for a single instrument or voice. In concertos the solo section is for the soloist; the *tutti* is for the complete orchestra.

sonata (IT. so-nah′tah) A composition commonly in three or four movements (sections), each complete in itself. The movements are contrasted in tempo, key, and mood.

C. P. E. Bach (1714–88) is usually considered the father of the modern sonata. His sonatas were in three movements: fast, slow, fast.

In the typical Beethoven sonata the movements are normally as follows:
1. First movement: usually in sonata form in a rapid tempo. See **sonata form.**
2. Second movement: usually slower and more expressive.
3. Third movement: minuet or scherzo.
4. Fourth movement: rondo or sonata form, in rapid tempo.

The word sonata comes from the Italian word *suonare,* which means "to sound." In early usage, sonata meant an instrumental piece, in contrast to cantata, which was a vocal piece.

sonata allegro form. See **sonata form.**

sonata form The form used for single movements of concertos, sonatas, symphonies, or chamber works. It is so commonly used for first movements that it is often called "first-movement form." The typical sonata form has three parts:
1. Exposition: states the themes around which the movement is built. In the classic sonata there are usually two themes or groups of themes, connected by a bridge passage and ending out of the original key. This section was generally repeated.
2. Development (often called "free fantasia"): freely develops and enlarges on the themes of the exposition.
3. Recapitulation: restatement of the main themes, but in the original (tonic) key. There is often an addition, the coda:
4. Coda: an extended ending.

sonatina   A short, simple sonata.

soprano   Highest of the voice ranges.

This is the range:

sordini (IT. sohr-dee′nee) The dampers of the piano. *Senza sordini* means to press down the sostenuto (damper) pedal. *Con sordini* means to release the sostenuto pedal.

sordino (IT. sohr-dee′noh) A wood or metal clip (mute) which is placed on the bridge of a stringed instrument to soften or mute the tone.

sospirando (IT. sos-peer-ahn′doh) Sighing; in a plaintive style.

sostenuto (IT. sos-tay-noo′toh) Sustained; hold for the full time value. Sostenuto sometimes means slightly slower, held back.

sotto (IT. soht′toh) Under. *Sotto voce* means "in an undertone," quietly.

space   The space between two lines of the staff.

There are four spaces on the staff: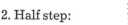

spinet
1. A harpsichord in a small four- or five-sided case. Like the virginal(s), it had one string to each note. See **harpsichord, virginal(s)**.
2. The name given to the modern small upright piano.

spiritoso (IT. spee-ree-toh′soh) Lively, spirited.

staccato (IT. stah-cah′toh) Sharply detached.

These are staccato signs:
Abbreviation: *stacc.*

staff

stave   Contains four spaces and five lines on which the notes are written to indicate pitch:

stem   The vertical line connected to a note head:

step   The movement of a melody from one note to its neighbor; a second.

There are three kinds of diatonic step:

1. Whole step:

2. Half step:

3. Augmented step:

There is one kind of chromatic half step:

See **diatonic** 2.

strepitoso (IT. stray-pee-toh′soh) Noisy.

stretto (IT. stret′toh)
1. In a fugue, the portion in which the subject and the answer follow so closely that they overlap. See **fugue**.
2. In a non-fugal composition, a concluding section in increased speed.

stringendo (IT. streen-jen′doh) Quickening. Abbreviation: *string.*

string quartet   Chamber music for four string instruments; usually two violins, viola, and violoncello. See **chamber music**.

string quintet   Chamber music for five string instruments. See **chamber music.**

subdominant   The fourth step of the major or minor scale; the subdominant chord is a triad built on this tone.

subito   (IT. soo′bee-toh)   Suddenly. 𝒑 *subito* means "suddenly soft."

subject   Theme or musical thought. A major idea on which a composition is built.

suite   (FR. sweet)

1. Instrumental music consisting of various movements, each one a different dance form, and all usually linked together by being in the same key. Such dance forms as the allemande, bourrée, courante, gavotte, gigue, minuet, and saraband appear in the classic suite.
2. A group of pieces in any style or form, often taken from operas, ballets, etc.

swing   See **jazz** 4.

symphony   A composition for orchestra resembling a sonata in structure, generally containing four movements.

Both the symphony and the sonata developed during the eighteenth century. The symphony was influenced by the Italian operatic overture, which was in three sections: fast, slow, fast. These sections were developed into separate movements. The addition of the minuet made the symphony a four-movement form. See **movement, sonata form.**

syncopation   The placing of an accent on a normally weak beat. This can be done in several ways:
1. A tie over the strong first beat:

2. An accent on a weak beat or between beats:

3. A rest on a strong beat:

4. A longer note on a weak beat:

T

tacet   (LAT. tass′et)   Silent.

tambourine   A percussion instrument. It consists of a wooden hoop with metal disc inserts called jingles, and is covered on one side with a drumhead. Single strokes are played by striking the drumhead with the knuckles. Rolls are produced by shaking the tambourine, or by rubbing the thumb along the drumhead, setting the jingles into motion.

tam-tam   A metal disc of saucer-like shape, struck with a heavy beater. Also called gong.

tango   A dance based on an African Negro dance, which later became popular in Spanish America, where it took on the rhythms and movements of a typical Spanish dance.

tarantella   (IT. tah-rahn-tel′lah)
tarantelle   (FR. tahr-ahn-tel)   An Italian dance in 6/8 time, constantly moving at a rapid speed.
It is believed that the tarantella was named after the tarantula, a poisonous spider whose bite was supposed to be cured by this dance. However, both the tarantella and the tarantula may have been named after the city of Taranto, a seaport in Southern Italy.

tempo Rate of speed, pace.
Some tempo marks are:
1. Slow: largo, grave, lento, adagio.
2. Moderate: andante, moderato.
3. Fast: allegro, vivace, presto.

tempo primo Return to original speed.

tenerezza (IT. tay-nare-ate′tsah) Tenderness.

tenor Highest natural male voice. This is the range:

tenor clef  C clef on the fourth line. Trombone and cello music is often written in this clef to avoid using leger lines. See **clef** 2.

tenor drum See **drum** 2.

tenuto (IT. tay-noo′toh) Held. The note is to be held for its full time value. This is a tenuto sign: Abbreviation: *ten.*

ternary Three part. In ternary form the first and third parts are usually alike. The middle part has a different melody and is often in a different key.

tetrachord The four scale tones that make up a perfect fourth. The major scale consists of two similar tetrachords (two whole steps and one half step):

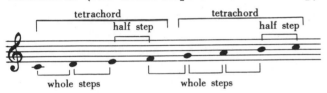

theme A complete musical idea; often used as a subject for variations.

third The interval of three diatonic tones.

This is a third:

See **interval.**

thirty-second note Thirty-two of these are equal to a whole note. Four thirty-second notes are equal to an eighth note.

thirty-second rest A measured silence equal to a thirty-second note.

TARANTELLE

tie A slur connecting two neighboring notes of the same pitch. The second note is not to be struck again, but is held for its full value:

time signature Shows the number of beats in a measure, and the kind of note that gets one beat:
3 three beats in the measure.
4 a quarter note gets one beat.

timpani (IT. tim′pah-nee) Also called kettledrum. See **drum** 4.

toccata (IT. toh-cah′tah) A piece for keyboard instrument having many bold, rapid passages, in a free, contrapuntal style.

tonic The first note of a scale; the keynote. The tonic chord is a triad built on this note. This is the tonic chord in the key of F:

tranquillo (IT. trahn-kweel′loh) Calm, quiet, tranquil.

transcription An arrangement of a musical composition for a voice or instrument other than that for which it originally was written.

transition

1. In musical form, a passage leading from one main section to another (for example, from the exposition to the development in the sonata).
2. A brief or passing modulation (change of key).

transpose To perform or write a piece in a key other than that in which it is written.

transposing instruments Instruments that produce a pitch different from that shown in the written music. Thus, music for these instruments is not written at the actual desired pitch. For example, the clarinet is built in B flat. If the player uses the fingering for D on the instrument, he produces the actual pitch of C, a whole step below.

traps The set of drums, cymbals, etc., used in dance bands.

treble The highest part of a choral or instrumental composition; soprano.

treble clef The G clef on the second line of the staff:

G line (G clef curls around the G line)

The treble clef in its present form developed out of the letter G. See **clef** 1.

tre corde (IT. tray core'day) See **una corda.**

triad (try'ad) A chord of three tones, consisting of a root, third, and fifth. Any triad may be inverted as follows:

triangle A percussion instrument. It is a steel bar bent in the shape of a triangle with one corner open. It is held by a string and struck with a metal bar. The triangle has a penetrating sound and is used sparingly.

trill Musical ornament that consists of a rapid alternation between a note and its upper neighbor. In the time of Bach and Handel, the trill was usually started on the neighbor note. In most later music, as in Chopin and Liszt, the trill is begun on the principal note.

These are trill signs:
See **ornaments.**

trio

1. Music for three performers.
2. The middle section of a minuet, march, or scherzo.

triple time Three beats to the measure; 3/8, 3/4, 3/2, etc.

triplet A group of three notes played in the same amount of time as two notes of the same kind:

tristo (IT. trees'toh) Sad.

trombone A brass wind instrument with cylindrical bore and a cup mouthpiece. Its chief characteristic is the slide, which can be lengthened so that any note within its range may be played. The slide takes the place of the valves used on most other brass instruments (however, valve trombones are sometimes used). The trombone developed from a large trumpet at the close of the fourteenth century.

The two types of trombone generally in use today are the tenor and bass. The trombone is not a transposing instrument, although it uses the tenor clef: in its highest register to avoid the use of leger lines.

This is the range of the tenor trombone:

This is the range of the bass trombone:

See **bore.**

MOUTHPIECE
BELL
SLIDE

troppo (IT. traw'poh) Too much. *Allegro ma non troppo* means "fast, but not too much so."

trumpet A brass wind instrument with cylindrical bore, cup mouthpiece, and three valves. The tone of the trumpet is brilliant and penetrating. The B flat trumpet is a transposing instrument.

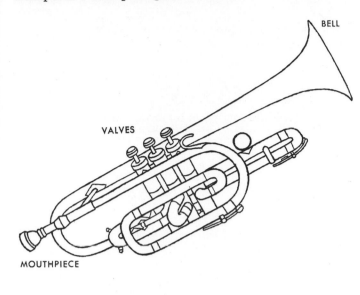

BELL

VALVES

MOUTHPIECE

This is its written range:

This is the actual sound:

See **transposing instruments, bore.**

tuba The lowest-pitched brass wind instrument.
1. The tuba has a conical bore, cup mouthpiece, and three or four valves. It is a descendant of the serpent, an ancient bass instrument. Tubas are built in E flat and BB flat (double B flat).
2. The sousaphone is a tuba in circular form developed for (and named after) John Philip Sousa. It is placed over the left shoulder while being played. The huge bell is detachable so that the sousaphone can be carried in a case.

The E flat tuba is written and sounds:

The BB flat tuba is written and sounds:
See **bore.**

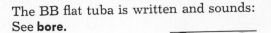

BELL

MOUTHPIECE

VALVES

tune Air, melody.

turn A turn is written:

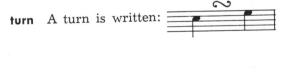

And played:

See **ornaments.**

tutti (IT. toot'ee) All.
1. The section of a composition in which all the instruments or voices perform.
2. In concertos, it is that section where the complete orchestra plays without the soloist.

tyrolienne (FR. tee-ro-l'yen) A Tyrolean folk song (and dance) in 3/4 time with rhythm similar to the ländler (an Austrian dance). It is sung with sudden vocal changes known as yodeling. See **falsetto, yodel.**

U

ukulele (you-ca-lay′lee) A four-stringed Hawaiian instrument of the guitar family, with a fretted finger board.

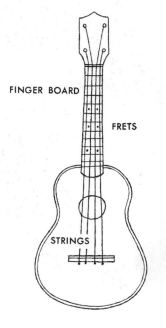

FINGER BOARD

FRETS

STRINGS

una corda (IT. oo′nah core′dah) Soft pedal; the left pedal on the piano which controls the hammers so that a soft tone is produced. Originally this pedal moved the entire action so that only one string was struck by the hammer instead of the usual two or three. (*Una corda* means "one string"). This principle of shifting the action is used in modern grand pianos. Abbreviation: *U.C.*
Tre corde means "three strings" or, without soft pedal.

unison The playing of the same pitch by several instruments or voices; also the playing of the same part an octave higher, called *all' unisono*.

upbeat An unaccented beat; begins a phrase or composition, often the last beat of a measure. In conducting, the upbeat is indicated by the upward motion of the hand.

V

valse (FR. vahls) Waltz. See **waltz**.

value The length of a note; time value.

valve A piston used in certain wind instruments. When pressed, it allows the air to travel through additional tubing, thus lengthening the vibrating air column, which lowers the pitch. Most brass instruments are equipped with valves, three being the standard number, although the lower brass instruments (baritone, euphonium, and tubas) sometimes have four.
In most brass instruments, the first valve lowers the pitch one whole step, the second valve by a half step, the third valve by one and one half steps. Combining these valves allows the performer to play any chromatic note within the range of the instrument.

vamp
1. To improvise an accompaniment (usually popular music).
2. An introductory section of two, four, or more measures before a solo or between verses while the soloist is preparing to sing or play.

variation A musical form. The theme is kept as the main idea but is varied through changes of key, meter, rhythm, harmony, speed, or mood.

veloce (IT. vay-loh′chay.) Rapid, swift.

vigoroso (IT. vee-goh-roh′soh) Energetic, vigorous.

viol (IT. vee'ole) A family of stringed instruments, played with a bow, popular during the sixteenth and seventeenth centuries; usually has six thin strings, a flat back, frets, and sloping shoulders. The tone is soft and delicate. The chief members of the family are: treble viol, tenor viol, and bass viol *(viola da gamba)*.

viola (IT. vee-oh'lah) A stringed instrument of the violin family, played with a bow; an alto violin. The viola is slightly larger than the violin, and is tuned a fifth lower. It is used chiefly in orchestra and chamber music. The tone is somewhat nasal. Music for the viola is written in the alto clef. See **bow**.

The four strings are tuned:

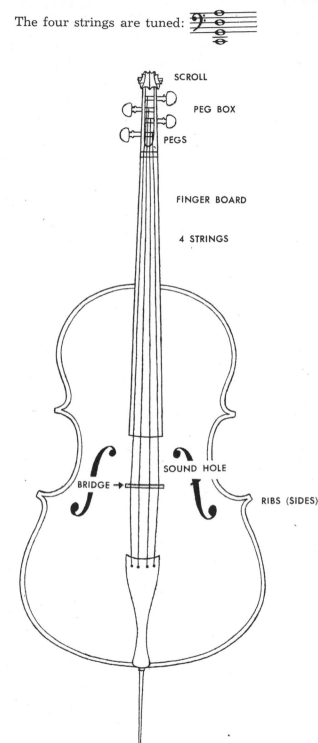

violin A stringed instrument, played with a bow. The violin is the most important orchestral instrument because of its expressiveness and tremendous range of tone qualities. See **bow**.

The four strings are tuned:

violoncello (IT. vee-oh-lon-chel'loh) A stringed instrument played with a bow. The cello (as the name is abbreviated) is similar to the violin in construction, but about double the length, and deeper from front to back. It is held between the knees while playing, and supported on the floor by a peg. The tone is much lower than the violin, with a rich, mellow quality.

The four strings are tuned:

SCROLL

PEG BOX

PEGS

FINGER BOARD

4 STRINGS

SOUND HOLE

BRIDGE →

RIBS (SIDES)

The cello bow is similar to the violin bow, but is shorter. See **bow**. Cello music is usually written in the bass clef, but is written in the tenor and treble clefs when it gets into the high ranges to avoid writing leger lines.

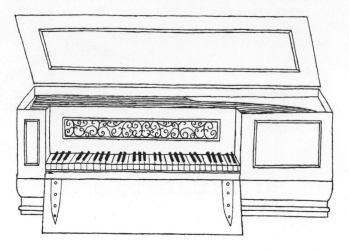

virginal(s) A keyboard instrument of the sixteenth and seventeenth centuries; a small harpsichord. The strings are at right angles to the keys, and are plucked by little rods called *virgulas,* from which the instrument may have gotten its name. There is one string for each note. Its tone is similar to that of the clavichord—delicate and sweet. Early virginals were small enough to be played while held on the lap; later, legs were added. The instrument usually has a range of four octaves. The name is written either virginal, or virginals, but in either case means only one instrument. See **harpsichord.**

virtuoso A performer with great technical skill.

vivace (IT. vee-vah'chay)
1. Lively, vivacious. *Allegro vivace* means livelier, or quicker than allegro.
2. Vivace alone means a speed faster than allegro, but not as fast as presto.

vivo (IT. vee'voh) Lively, vivacious.

vocal music Music for voice or voices.

voce (IT. vo'chay)
voice
1. Sound produced by the vocal cords.
2. One of the parts in a vocal or instrumental composition, such as the bass voice of a choral composition.

volante (IT. voh-lahn'tay) Rapidly; "flying."

volti subito (IT. vohl'tee soo'bee-toh) Turn (the page) quickly. Abbreviation: *V.S.*

W

waltz A dance of German origin, in 3/4 time. The waltz became popular around 1800, and has been danced ever since. It varied in tempo from slow to moderately fast. The waltz developed from the ländler (an Austrian peasant dance), and was one of the first dances in which the partners embraced each other.

whole note Equals four quarter notes.

whole rest

1. A measured silence equal to a whole note.
2. A complete measure's rest in any time signature.

whole step See **step** 1.

wind instruments Instruments whose tones are produced by an enclosed, vibrating column of air.
There are two main types of wind instruments:
1. Brass family— instruments made of brass or other metal: baritone, bugle, cornet, French horn, mellophone, trombone, trumpet, tuba, etc.
2. Woodwind family— instruments made of wood (although some are now made of metal as well): bassoon, clarinet, English horn, flute, oboe, piccolo, etc. The flute and piccolo are now more commonly made of metal, but are still classed as woodwinds.
The organ and accordion may also be considered wind instruments.

woodwind family See **wind instruments** 2.

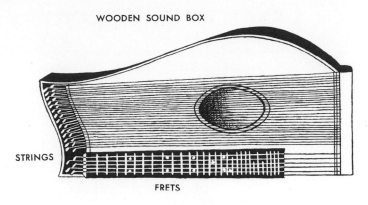

WOODEN SOUND BOX

STRINGS

FRETS

X

xylophone (zy'loh-fone) Percussion instrument. A set of tuned wooden bars arranged like a piano keyboard, with a hollow tube (resonator) under each bar; played with wooden hammers. The xylophone has a range of about four octaves. See **marimba.**

Y

yodel A type of singing without words popular among the mountain folk of Switzerland and Austria. It is characterized by a frequent and sudden change from low chest tones to high falsetto tones. See **falsetto.**

Z

zither A stringed instrument. The zither consists of a flat wooden sound box over which twenty-seven to forty-five strings may be stretched. Four or five melody strings, placed over a fretted finger board, are plucked with a metal ring (plectrum) worn on the right thumb. The other strings are plucked with the fingers, and are used for the accompaniment. The zither is very popular in Bavaria and Austria. See **autoharp.**

TABLE OF MUSICAL SIGNS

Accidentals

sharp   ♯

double sharp   ✕

flat   ♭

double flat   ♭♭

natural   ♮

Bars

bar line |

double bar   ‖

final double bar   ‖

Clefs

G clef (treble)

F clef (bass)

C clef (alto)

C clef (tenor)

Dynamics

fortissimo   *ff*

forte   *f*

mezzo forte   *mf*

mezzo piano   *mp*

piano   *p*

pianissimo   *pp*

crescendo   ⟨

decrescendo   ⟩

accents

Octave signs

8va----------

8----------

Ornaments

acciaccatura

appoggiatura (long)

arpeggio

grace note

inverted mordent   ∿

mordent   ∿

trill   *tr* ∿∿

turn   ∽

Pedal

℘ed.   ✳

Repeats   ‖: :‖

D.C. al fine

D.C. al segno

D.S.

Rests

whole rest   ▬

half rest   ▬

quarter rest   𝄽

eighth rest   𝄾

sixteenth rest   𝄿

thirty-second rest   𝅀

sixty-fourth rest   𝅁

Rhythm

fermata   𝄐

tie

triplet

4/4 time   **C**

2/2 time   ¢

Style

legato

portamento

staccato

TABLE OF MUSICAL ABBREVIATIONS

accel.	accelerando		*m.g.*	main gauche
accomp.	accompaniment		*M.M.*	Maelzel metronome
ad lib.	ad libitum		*mp*	mezzo piano
allarg.	allargando		*Op.*	opus
cresc.	crescendo		*Ped., P*	pedal
D.C.	da capo		*p*	piano
decresc.	decrescendo		*pp*	pianissimo
dim., dimin.	diminuendo		*pizz.*	pizzicato
D.S.	dal segno		*rall.*	rallentando
espress.	espressivo		*rf, rfz, rinf.*	rinforzando
f	forte		*r.h.*	right hand
ff	fortissimo		*rit., ritard.*	ritardando
fp	forte piano		*riten.*	ritenuto
fz	forzando		*sf, sfz*	sforzando
gliss.	glissando		*sim.*	simile
leg.	legato		*smorz.*	smorzando
legg.	leggiero		*stacc.*	staccato
l.h.	left hand		*string.*	stringendo
marc.	marcato		*ten.*	tenuto
m.d. {	mano destra, main droite		*tr*	trill
			U.C.	una corda
mf	mezzo forte		*V.S.*	volti subito